W9-BSJ-328

© 2005 Hallmark Licensing, Inc.
www.hallmark.com

All rights reserved. No part of this publication may be reproduced or transmitted in any form or by any means, electronic or mechanical, including photocopying, recording, or any other information storage and retrieval system, without the written permission of the publisher.

Editorial Director: Todd Hafer
Art Director: Kevin Swanson
Editor: Jeff Morgan

Design: Christine Taylor
Illustration: Peg Carlson-Hoffman
Handlettering: MyDung Cong
Production Art: Dan C. Horton

Printed and bound in China

ISBN: 1-59530-111-9

First Edition, September 2005

10 9 8 7 6 5 4 3 2 1

On a personal note

A GUIDE TO WRITING NOTES WITH STYLE

BY ANGELA ENSMINGER & KEELY CHACE

On a personal note

A GUIDE TO WRITING NOTES WITH STYLE

BY ANGELA ENSMINGER & KEELY CHACE

contents:

personal notes from the authors

Hi Everybody,

The fact that you bought this book says one very important thing…you've got great intentions. Now, you also have two people who know a little about writing who are going to walk you through the creepy back alleys of note writing and help you turn those great intentions into really great notes.

Writing this book has made me a better note writer, too, so I'm excited for you to give it a try. I really hope you like it. I also hope you'll get in touch with Keely and me and let us know what you think! Because not only do we like writing notes (and writing books about writing notes), we like getting them, too!

Congratulations on taking the initiative and getting this book. Now all that's left to do is write your own really great notes.

All the best,

Angela Ensminger

Angela Ensminger

Dear Reader,

This note is just to say I hope you find this book useful, friendly, and maybe even a little inspiring. Angela and I wrote it with the goal of alleviating some of the anxiety that seems to go hand in hand with writing personal notes. We've filled these pages with helpful tips and ideas to make note writing a more effortless and rewarding way to take care of all your relationships.

You can do this. You can write caring, meaningful notes that reflect your tastes and personality, and this book can help. I hope you'll use this book until every last page is dog-eared and ink-stained, and I hope you have a lot of fun along the way!

Sincerely,

Keely Chace

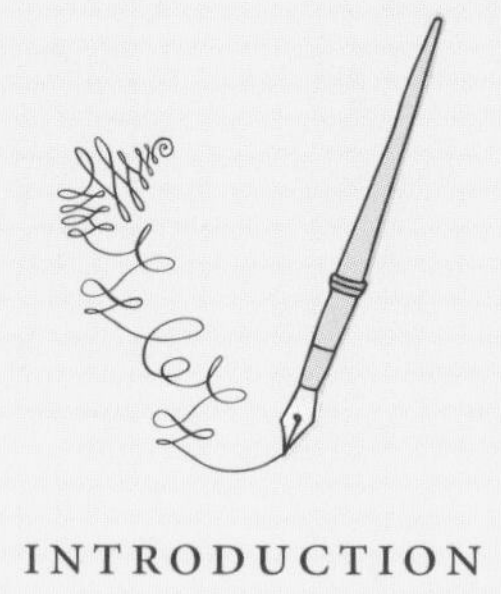

INTRODUCTION

why *personal* notes matter

There are quicker, more convenient options, right? We can e-mail. We can call. We can text message. We can instant message. We can even talk face to face. And the other options take about a second compared with sitting down and writing a note. While we don't believe that writing a note is going to replace any of these ways of communicating, we also don't believe that the other ways could ever replace writing a meaningful and personal note.

Most of us can agree that life presents us with occasions when only the kind of messages people can hold in their hands and keep forever will do—and plenty of other occasions when writing that kind of message is simply a nice thing to do.

So let's consider a note a more personal, permanent supplement to e-mails and phone calls, a way of broadening our communication options. When we write one, we're going the extra mile to show we care. When someone receives one, she can tell we really put something of ourselves into it—our time, our thought, our effort, our tastes, our personality.

In a nutshell, great personal notes tell people they matter to us, that we took the time to sit down and write just to them, that we didn't go for the easiest option, that they are worth our time.

Now what's more personal than that? And, sure, it might take a little longer to sit down and write one...but it'll be worth it. You'll see.

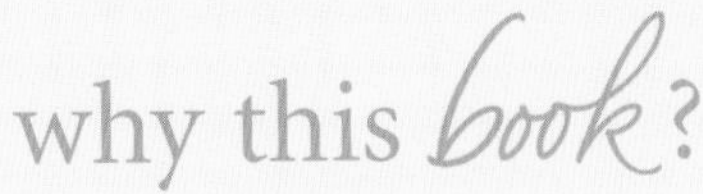

why this book?

THIS BOOK WAS WRITTEN WITH ONE GOAL IN MIND—HELPING YOU WRITE NOTES THAT YOU FEEL GREAT ABOUT. IT'S THAT SIMPLE.

And while it offers plenty of good, solid information—including the six steps to writing notes for every occasion, as well as useful tips and extra inspiration throughout—this book doesn't get hung up on hard-and-fast rules or on the "art" of note writing. That's just not us.

In fact, this book is much more about the heart of note writing, about why we want to write in the first place, about how good it feels to find the right words to express ourselves and how great it is to know those words are going to matter to someone.

It's also about sitting down and knowing you're going to write a great note. If you want to know how that feels, this book is for you. Plus, we think you'll really like it and use it. And that makes us feel good, too.

So here's to writing notes with personality and style.
Here's to you!

how to use this *book*

READ THIS...BECAUSE WE WANT YOU TO KNOW HOW TO USE THIS BOOK.

Certain occasions call for certain kinds of notes. When those occasions arise, the last thing we want to do is hunt around for the information we need to write a great note! So we've made it easy for you by organizing this book according to common note-writing occasions. When you need to say thanks, just flip to the Gratitude chapter.

Each chapter takes a great note and breaks it down into little can-do steps. We walk you through each step with tips to inspire and guide you. We give you sample notes—then go on to explain what makes them so great, so you'll be ready to start writing in no time. That said, if you want to jump straight into note writing, we've also included words and phrases and additional sample notes that you can just plain copy.

And for those of you who want to keep this book up on a high shelf somewhere, please don't. This book was made to be used—and used often. It might even be a good idea to keep it together with pens, blank notes, and stamps, so when you need to write, you'll be all set.

So go ahead. Don't worry about being gentle. Flip through, bookmark, dog-ear the pages. You can even write in it, underline parts, or circle stuff if you want. This book can take it. It won't mind at all. And as long as you keep writing great notes, we won't either. Promise.

contents:

Gratitude

It's usually pretty easy to get those first few words out... *Thank you for*...but then we're faced with The Big Umm. We know we should say more, but what?

Let's face it, thank-you notes are the single most common type of note we write. In fact, writing them is such an important life skill that there should have been a "Great Thank-You Note Writing" class in school! Instead, we practiced our penmanship while the words we had to write were left up to us. But all shoulds, coulds, and woulds aside—knowing how to write a great thank-you note is a skill worth learning, no matter your age. A little guidance and practice are all it takes to get the hang of it. If only great penmanship were that simple.

CHAPTER INTRODUCTION

why *thank-you* notes matter

Whether it's a present, a party, a heart-to-heart talk, or a favor—when people do something nice for us, they're giving us the gifts of their thought and time. And a really great thank-you note recognizes this. It does more than just thank people for what they did. It also expresses gratitude for what went into doing it. It's the best way (*and sometimes the only way*) to return their kindness. Great thank-you notes tell people that what they did—as well as how and why they did it—matters to us.

6 parts of a *thank-you* note

A thank-you note consists of six simple parts, so writing a great one is as easy as 1-2-3 (well, 1-2-3-4-5-6, actually).

① *Dear Louise,*

② *Thank you so much for the beautiful sweater you gave me for my birthday!* ③ *Blue is my favorite color (as you apparently know!), and there's just nothing better than a cozy wool sweater on a cold day. I look forward to wearing it during the rest of our cold winter here.* ④ *It means a lot that you thought of me on my birthday…you're such a good friend. I hope we can meet for lunch soon.* ⑤ *Thank you again for your thoughtful gift!*

⑥ *Fondly,*
Leslie

① GREET THE RECIPIENT
② EXPRESS YOUR GRATITUDE
③ ELABORATE
④ COMPLIMENT & LOOK AHEAD
⑤ RESTATE YOUR GRATITUDE
⑥ GIVE YOUR REGARDS

great *thank-you* notes: step by step

① GREET THE RECIPIENT

Great thank-you notes start off right.

- Don't forget to double-check that you're using the correct form and spelling of the recipient's name, as well as the names of others mentioned in your note.
- Be sure to use the right level of formality. In doubt? If you don't know the recipient well enough to address her by only her first name, use the more formal last name with the correct title (*Mr., Mrs., Miss, Dr., etc.*).

② EXPRESS YOUR GRATITUDE

The body of great thank-you notes begins with those two magical words, *Thank You.*

- Clearly state your thanks, then enhance and personalize them.
- Try adding adjectives (*see lists on pages 27, 35 and 43*) to describe the gift or event and your positive reaction to it.
- Phrases like *I simply love it!* or *What a wonderful time!* add warmth and enthusiasm to your note.
- For more formal thank-you notes, keep it simple and to the point.

③ ELABORATE

Great thank-you notes use specific details to let your recipient know she's made a lasting impression with her kindness.

- For a gift, take the opportunity to tell her your plans for it, or if you're already using it, tell her how.
- For events, call out something specific you enjoyed, or let her know what stands out in your mind now that it's over.
- To thank someone for lending her ears or time, tell her how much better you're feeling now or how much she helped you out.

④ COMPLIMENT & LOOK AHEAD

Great thank-you notes make people feel good about themselves and their relationship with you.

- Compliment her on her thoughtfulness, and if you're comfortable doing so, remind her of the special place she holds in your life.
- Mention the next time you might see or talk to her. If that's not an option, let her know you're thinking of her.
- In a more formal note, let her know you appreciate her time and look forward to speaking with, meeting with, or hearing from her again.

TIMING

A good rule of thumb: Timeliness equals thoughtfulness. Try to send your note within three days of an event or receipt of a gift, while the event or gift is still fresh in your mind (*and the recipient's, too*). That said, late is still better than never. If your note will arrive more than a week after an event or a gift's arrival, apologize for the delay, but don't dwell on it. Use humor if you like. People will understand.

⑤ RESTATE YOUR GRATITUDE

Great thank-you notes come full circle and end the way they begin—by saying thanks.

- Briefly and simply reiterate your gratitude from your first line.
- Consider quick but creative ways to round out your thanks by adding a little color, detail, or description, like *Thanks for brightening my day* or *Thank you so much—you're an angel!*

⑥ GIVE YOUR REGARDS

Great notes end with an appropriate closing.

- Choose your closing carefully, depending on the recipient.
- *Sincerely* is a good general closing.
- For closer relationships, consider warmer closings such as *Fondly* or *Love*.
- For casual relationships, it's always OK to simply sign your name.

You'll find lots of options for regards in the Great Endings section on page 216.

3 THANK-YOU THOUGHTS TO REMEMBER...

Thank-you notes are like outfits—certain kinds are suited for certain occasions. Some are like jeans; others are like tuxedos, so be sure to match your words (*and your paper*!) to the occasion.

It's easier to whip up a cake if you keep flour, eggs, and sugar on hand. The same goes for thank-you notes—so be sure to keep a variety of notes, envelopes, stamps, and writing instruments together and handy so you're ready to write a great note any time.

A thank-you note on someone's mail stack is like the cherry on top of a sundae. She might go for it first. She might want to save it for last. Either way, she's sure to enjoy it...so feel good about writing and sending one.

SECTION NO. 1

thank-you notes for gifts

Some gifts are just what we wanted. Others, well…aren't. But in all cases, gift givers spent time and energy trying to get us something we'd like. And that deserves our thanks.

There is more to thank-you notes for gifts than meets the eye. They not only let people know that their gift is appreciated, arrived intact, or works well, but that their effort really means something to us. And our notes can include lots of details and personal touches, so even if some gifts may not reflect our style exactly…our thank-you notes always can!

REASONS FOR SENDING

For some of these gifts, thanks are expected. For others, simply saying thanks is customary...but wouldn't a note be a great surprise?

- Birthday gifts
- Holiday gifts (*Christmas, Father's Day*)
- Wedding and bridal shower gifts
- Baby gifts
- Graduation gifts
- Gifts for religious rites of passage
- Housewarming, hostess, and hospitality gifts
- Yummy things given from someone's kitchen
- Articles sent, magazines or books shared

TIMING

Do your best to be a good recipient and send your thank-you note as soon as possible after receiving a gift. The standard three-day rule applies. If you wait longer, try not to let more than a week go by, and be sure to tell the recipient how you've been using the gift or what plans you have for it.

PS: Thank-You Notes for Wedding Gifts Have Their Own Rules...

Don't panic, because for wedding gifts, a three-month rule, rather than three-day rule, applies! This traditional rule is a good one to keep in mind: Wedding thank-you notes should be sent within three months of the receipt of a gift, not the ceremony itself.

4 great *thank-you* notes for gifts

Notes like this will warm Nana's heart for the next few years, until Madison is able to write thank-you notes herself. It sounds like Grandma doesn't get to see her granddaughter very often, so she's sure to appreciate hearing that Madison knows who the gift is from and is enjoying it so much.

Dear Nana,

Thank you so much for the toy baby bottles you sent Madison for her birthday. I remember playing with some just like them when I was little, and I think Madison is having just as much fun. When I ask her who they're from, she lights up and says, "Nana!" They were really thoughtful and sweet things for you to send. We both can't wait to visit you this summer. Thanks again, Nana!

Love you,
Alicia

It's good note-writing etiquette to mention the amount of money (cash, check, or gift card) someone gave you as a gift. If that makes you uncomfortable, however, you can simply state, "Thank you for your generous check." Be sure to let people know, as Aaron does here, what you plan to spend it on. Aaron's energy and detail will make Mr. and Mrs. Lopez feel like they picked the perfect gift (*without actually having to pick*).

Dear Mr. and Mrs. Lopez,

Thank you for the $50 check you sent for my high school graduation. What a generous gift! I'm taking a two-week trip to Mexico this summer, and I'm planning to use the money toward my airfare. I'm so excited about the trip, and this really helps out! It means a lot that you thought of me on my big day. I'll be sure to send you a picture from my trip. Thank you again!

Sincerely,
Aaron Fuentes

Dear Aunt Sharon and Uncle Bob,

We absolutely love the beautiful table you gave us as a wedding gift… Thank you! It looks great in our living room, and it's really making our new house feel like home! We are so overwhelmed by your generosity and by all the effort that must have gone into choosing something that fits our taste so well! Having you there to celebrate our special day meant so much to us both. We look forward to seeing you next month at Lucy's party. Thanks again for such a wonderful gift.

With love,
Nikki and Matt

The note is signed "Nikki and Matt" and is written from both people who are using the gift. Though tradition calls for one person to write (*and sign*) a note in the name of the couple, this modern approach is a perfectly appropriate way for a couple to express their thanks. It's warm and really lets Uncle Bob and Aunt Sharon know how much their gift and attendance at the wedding were appreciated.

Dear Judy,

Thanks for the gorgeous yellow daffodils from your garden. What a nice surprise to come to work on Monday and find that spring had come to my desk! It's nice to work with someone so thoughtful.

Thanks for brightening my day—I'll see you at lunch.

Gratefully,
Connie

A quick thank-you to a co-worker for a surprising "just because" gift will let her know it is appreciated. Now the nice surprises are going both ways!

writing your *thank-you* note

NEED TO SAY THANKS BUT DON'T KNOW WHERE TO BEGIN? START BY ANSWERING THE QUESTIONS BELOW:

How did you feel when you opened the gift?

What words describe the gift itself? The thought behind it?

What are you doing with the gift now? Any future plans for it?

Why is this a good gift for you?

Does the gift commemorate something? Is it sentimental?

Does the gift make something in your life easier, prettier, better?

Had you seen something like it and thought you'd like to have it?

Does the gift remind you of the giver when you see it?

Did the giver have to go to extra effort to make, find, or purchase the gift?

If it is a gift of money (*or a gift card*), how do you plan to use it?

NEED MORE INSPIRATION? We've included additional sample notes at the end of this chapter.

Now, following the steps on pages 18-20, use your answers—along with the words and phrases on the following pages—to create a note that puts your thanks into words!

some of our favorite words for gift *thank-you* notes

Generous
Thoughtful
Creative
Unique
Meaningful
Perfect
Surprising
Beautiful
Cute
Fabulous
Useful
Practical
Appreciated
Touching
Luxurious
Fantastic
Just My Taste
Sweet
Kind
Impressive
Heartwarming
Loving
Sensational
Stylish
Love-Filled
Much-Needed
Considerate

a few great phrases for gift *thank-you* notes

How did you know (Sumatra) *was my favorite* (coffee)*?*

You have such great taste!

What a (thoughtful, generous, fun) *gift!*

I really appreciate it.

The time it must have taken you to (make it, find it)!

It really made my day!

It means so much to me.

It reminds me of (our annual trip to the beach house).

I have it sitting on my (kitchen table) *right now.*

Every time I (see it, wear it, use it) *I'll think of you.*

I'm looking forward to using it for (my trip to Chicago).

It's one of the most (touching, luxurious) *gifts I've ever received!*

YOUR NOTE IS REALLY GOING TO BRIGHTEN SOMEONE'S DAY WHEN...

The recipient feels good because she can picture the vase she gave you sitting on your table or you wearing the scarf she crocheted for you.

The note is so "you" that she feels like she's spoken with you after reading it.

She feels like an exceptional gift giver after reading it—especially when it comes to you—and she can't wait to find something else for you!

SECTION NO. 2

thank-you notes for support & acts of kindness

Some of the things we're most grateful for aren't "things" at all. They're words and kindnesses that come just when we need them most. They are intangible gifts—and they deserve our generous thanks.

Great thank-you notes for support and acts of kindness acknowledge the time and effort that went into the support we've received and make it clear that we feel better because of them. And because these thank-you notes are often unexpected, they can truly make people feel good about what they've done.

REASONS FOR SENDING

For Acts of Service, Favors, and Help

Thanks are in order for helpful acts, big and small, such as:

House-sitting, pet-sitting, and baby-sitting.

The use of equipment, vehicle, house, vacation home.

Lending a hand with errands, moving, or transportation.

Giving advice, suggestions, or tips.

Assisting with projects, tasks, or event planning.

Tutoring or mentoring children.

For Emotional Support During Difficult Times

Consider sending a thank-you note for help or encouragement received:

During an illness or recovery from an injury or surgery.

After a divorce or breakup.

For work problems or job loss.

While experiencing family issues.

While adjusting to life with a new baby.

For Expressions of Sympathy

When someone dies, people often reach out with support and kindness. Sending thank-you notes to people who've done so is a customary way to recognize such thoughtfulness. Notes should be sent after a funeral by the deceased's immediate family to people who sent mass or sympathy cards, flowers, meals, made donations, ran errands, helped with the ceremony, or offered other assistance. In the case of death following a prolonged illness, support offered during the illness should also be acknowledged.

TIMING

If you can follow the standard three-day rule, try to do so. But, because these notes are often occasioned by difficult times, the better-late-than-never rule applies more than ever. People will understand if it takes you a while to write a note. Just do it as soon as you are able, ideally while what they did for you is still fresh in your mind.

4 great *thank-you* notes for support & acts of kindness

Ellen warmly thanks her neighbor, with whom she seems not to be on a first-name basis, for her time and trouble and makes a specific offer to return the favor.

Dear Ms. Garcia,

Thank you so much for taking such good care of our house while we were in Mexico this past week. I know that you had to go out of your way to look after so much—especially our garden and letting Pepper out three times a day! I hope you know how much we appreciate your help. You're a wonderful neighbor! We're more than happy to return the favor when your vacation time comes. Thanks again for everything.

Sincerely,
Ellen Chase

Judging by the amount of help that Beth gave Jenn, it's likely that they are family or very close friends. Their closeness also comes through in informal touches like the short names used (*"Beth" for Elizabeth, "Jenn" for Jennifer*) and, of course, the warm closing (*Love*). Jenn also nurtures the relationship by acknowledging that Beth made sacrifices to help, even though she had her own family to take care of.

Dear Beth,

I can't thank you enough for all the help you gave us after Ethan was born. Although it's taken me a while to write, I really appreciate the time you took to bring meals and help out with laundry—especially when you have a family of your own to take care of. I hope you can come over to visit soon—you'll be amazed at how far we've come since those nervous first days! Again, Beth, thanks. You're an angel!

Love,
Jenn

Dear Mr. and Mrs. Cohen,

On behalf of my mother, my two brothers, and our families, I want to thank you for the touching card and beautiful flowers you sent following the loss of my father. It meant a lot to us to have you honor his memory in such a thoughtful way. We especially liked the story you shared in your card about Dad's famous practical jokes. It really is a comfort to know that you have such good memories of him, too.

We truly appreciate your thoughtfulness.

Sincerely,
Jessica Levin

It's common for a sympathy thank-you note to be written by one person "on behalf of" her family, as we see here. The formality of this note is appropriate for the occasion. Jessica's note expresses the gratitude the rest of her family feels but might not be able to write yet, and importantly, it lets the Cohens know that what they did was comforting and appreciated.

Hi, Jason,

I want to say thanks for being there for me since my layoff last month. I really appreciate the time you've taken to listen and to help me see that losing my job is not the end of the world. Thanks to you, I'm feeling much better, and I'm actually starting to think this could be a good thing. And no matter what the future holds, I'm keeping our weekly golf game on my calendar! Thanks for being such a good friend.

Sincerely,
Nathan

This is a real "blue jeans" thank-you, from the casual greeting to the conversational language used throughout. While Nathan's future thank-you note to a potential employer following a job interview will surely be much more formal than this, between close friends this kind of casual sincerity is just fine.

writing your *thank-you* note

READY TO GET STARTED? ASK YOURSELF THESE QUESTIONS:

What exactly was done for you? Why does it deserve special thanks?

How did the timing of the kindness make things better for you?

How did you feel when you received the support or help?

Was the support or help unexpected?

Has the support or help made something in your life easier, nicer, better?

Did the person who helped have to go out of her way to do it?

Did her support or help impact more people than just you? Who?

What qualities must she have in order to do what she did for you?

Is there something specific you'd like to do for her to say thank you?

Now, following the steps on pages 18-20, use your answers to the questions put your thanks into words. Great words and phrases are listed on the following pages to point you in the right direction. Next thing you know, you're going to have a great thank-you note!

NEED MORE INSPIRATION?
We've included additional sample notes at the end of this chapter.

some of our favorite words for support & kindness *thank-you* notes

ABOUT THE PERSON:

Kind	*Cheerful*	*Caring*	*Understanding*
Compassionate	*Considerate*	*Loving*	*Great*
Thoughtful	*Willing*	*Supportive*	*Sweet*

ABOUT WHAT THE PERSON DID:

Welcome	*Generous*	*Unexpected*	*Heartwarming*
Helpful	*Wonderful*	*Touching*	*Encouraging*
Much-Needed	*Important*	*Timely*	*Invaluable*

ABOUT HOW IT MADE YOU FEEL:

Grateful	*Relieved*	*Rested*	*Optimistic*
Supported	*Happy*	*Better*	*Listened To*
Cared About	*Touched*	*Hopeful*	*Calm*

a few great phrases for support & kindness *thank-you* notes

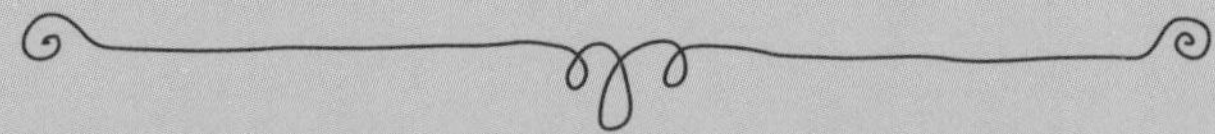

I can't thank you enough for (helping us move).

I really appreciate the time you took to (have coffee and talk yesterday).

Your help not only meant a lot to me, but also (to the kids).

You're a wonderful friend.

Your (advice) *has really stuck with me.*

(Your story about Jill) *really helped put things into perspective for me.*

I'm feeling so much better now.

Your support helped make a difficult time a lot easier.

It really helped not to have to worry about (making dinner).

Your fond memories of (Janice) *really touched our hearts.*

The outpouring of (support and love) *was overwhelming.*

(Our mother) *would have truly appreciated the* (beautiful lilies).

YOUR NOTE IS GOING TO MAKE SOMEONE FEEL BETTER WHEN...

The recipient can tell how much her gesture meant to you.

She would gladly provide help, support, and encouragement to you again.

She feels like an even better person after reading it.

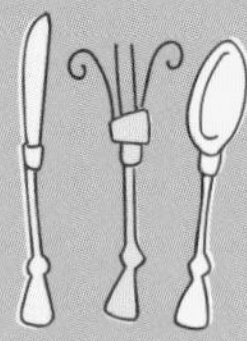

SECTION NO. 3

thank-you notes for social events & hospitality

Our social calendars fill up. Our "to do" lists grow long. There's simply not enough time to write thank-you notes. Sound familiar? Even though our lives are busier than ever these days, remember this: Writing really great thank-you notes is the best way to make sure our social calendars continue to fill up.

At their heart, great thank-you notes for social events and hospitality return a little of the graciousness we were treated to. They say, *I enjoyed myself. Thanks for having me.* They acknowledge the effort someone went to on our behalf. And if we consider the time and effort someone took to entertain us or open her home to us, writing her a great thank-you note should seem like no big to-do at all.

REASONS FOR SENDING

Whether a dinner, an overnight visit, a party in your honor, or another event, be a great guest and always let your host or hostess know how grateful you are.

Parties or Events Attended

Did you have a good time? Let the host know! Consider thank-yous for:

- Birthday parties
- Dinner parties
- Anniversary celebrations
- Barbecues or other casual get-togethers

Parties Thrown for You

Guests of honor owe their hosts a hearty thank-you.

- Surprise parties
- Bridal or couples showers, bachelor or bachelorette parties
- Baby Showers
- Going away, anniversary, or retirement celebrations

Hospitality

Did someone go out of his or her way for you? Say thanks.

- Overnight stays in someone's home
- Meals in someone's home
- Restaurant meals, especially when someone else pays

TIMING

The standard three-day rule applies. If you can't manage that, try to send your thank-you within a week of the event or hospitality. But do send a note even if it's later than that. Your hostess will still appreciate hearing how much you liked the decadent chocolate cake at her party or the beautiful quilt in her guest room.

PS: What if it was awful?

Even if you didn't enjoy the party or the overnight stay, you can still thank someone for having you and for the time and effort that went into it. Be grateful for your hostess's time and effort, then try and pick out something you did like and focus on that. Remember—even if it was awful, good manners still apply.

4 great *thank-you* notes for social events & hospitality

Perhaps Eric doesn't know Mrs. Conti well because he starts off his note by addressing her by her title and last name. And not only did he enjoy her home and her cooking, he liked the sausage stuffing in particular. This kind of detail sounds very appreciative and sincere. A compliment to not only Mrs. Conti, but also to her family at the note's end, wraps up his thanks perfectly.

Dear Mrs. Conti,

Thank you for having me as a guest in your home over Thanksgiving. Your house is so warm and comfortable that I felt right at home. Thanksgiving dinner was great, too. John was right—you are a fantastic cook. Your sausage stuffing was one of the best things I've ever tasted! It was great to spend the holiday with such a fun family. Thank you for all you did to make my stay so nice.

Sincerely,
Eric DeGangi

In this warm, appreciative note from one friend to another, Teresa expresses gratitude for Gail's preparations, acknowledges the thoughtful touches and hard work, and compliments the great results. Even better, she makes a very specific offer to return the favor. "Blessings" works as a closing because Teresa knows Gail is comfortable with it.

Dear Gail,

Thank you for the wonderful bridal shower you hosted for me! Everything was perfect—the flowers, the finger foods, and especially the cheesecake! I know you went to a lot of trouble to pull everything together. I can't wait to return the favor by hosting your baby shower in August! Thanks again for all you did to make the shower such a good time for everyone, especially me. You're a great friend.

Blessings,
Teresa

Dear Luis and Rita,

Thank you so much for inviting us to your 40th anniversary celebration! We were touched that you included us. It was such a beautiful evening, and we enjoyed meeting your family so much, especially Luis's Uncle Ignacio. What a character! Also, it was a pleasure to hear all the toasts and stories…what wonderful tributes to the life you've made together. Again, thank you for sharing your special occasion with us. Here's to many more happy years!

Sincerely,
Linda and Dale Peterson

Linda and Dale seem to be tickled pink just to have been invited. What a bonus that the party was so enjoyable! Specific compliments on the couple's family and the evening's events round out this gracious, friendly, and upbeat note.

Dear Susan,

Thank you for inviting Sophie and me to Zach's birthday party. Zach looked so cute in his cowboy outfit, and The Pizza Palace was a great place for all the kids. The party favor box has been a big hit with Sophie. She's used up all the stickers, and she loves the sidewalk chalk! I'm so glad that Sophie's in school with such great kids, and I'm having fun getting to know all the moms, too. Thanks for inviting us! See you at preschool drop-off.

Sincerely,
Julianne

This is a note that works great even if the party itself wasn't so hot. By commenting on a few key details (*Zach looked cute, the location was perfect, the party favors were great*) Julianne focuses on the positive and nurtures a relationship for herself and for her daughter in the process.

writing your *thank-you* note

THANKS ARE IN ORDER!
TO GET STARTED, ANSWER THE QUESTIONS BELOW:

What words come to mind when you remember the event?

How did it feel to be at the location of the event or visit?

Did the host do something special to make you comfortable?

Was there a meal? Drinks? Special dish? Dessert?

Was there a particularly great conversation that stands out in your mind?

What did your host do well that you really admired or enjoyed?

How did you feel when the event or visit was over?

How long had it been since you saw the host or the other guests?

Is there another event happening soon to look forward to?

Do you want to reciprocate? If so, how?

By referring to the steps on pages 18-20 and using your answers to these questions, as well as the words and phrases on the following pages, you'll be ready to build your thank-you note.

WANT TO SEE MORE SAMPLE NOTES?
We've included more for you at the end of this chapter.

some of our favorite words for social events & hospitality *thank-you* notes

ABOUT THE HOSTESS:

Gracious	*Engaging*	*Generous*	*Welcoming*
Well-Prepared	*Creative*	*Warm*	*Thorough*
Accommodating	*Thoughtful*	*Kind*	*Witty*

ABOUT THE EVENT OR HOSPITALITY:

Enjoyable	*Perfect*	*Fun*	*Restful*
Well-Planned	*Lively*	*Pleasant*	*Wonderful*
Unforgettable	*Comfortable*	*Beautiful*	*Superb*

ABOUT YOUR FEELINGS:

Pampered	*Thankful*	*Welcome*	*Delighted*
Appreciative	*Excited*	*Pleased*	*Comfortable*
Honored	*Happy*	*Grateful*	*Impressed*

a few great phrases for social events & hospitality *thank-you* notes

Thank you for inviting me and for also including (my friend Phillip).

I was so (happy) *to be there.*

Thank you for your hospitality.

I really appreciate all you did to make me feel so welcome.

It was wonderful.

I particularly enjoyed (the crème brûlée).

I really enjoyed myself.

Your home is lovely!

I can't remember the last time I had so much fun!

From start to finish, (the evening) *was absolutely perfect.*

It was such a pleasure to talk with you and your guests.

It was good to (see you, catch up with you).

YOUR THANKS WILL REALLY HIT HOME WHEN...

The recipients laugh about a funny conversation all over again.

They feel great about their home or party-planning abilities.

They would gladly invite you back to their home or to their next celebration.

sample *thank-you* notes for gifts

WARM
FOR GIFT

Dear Auntie Lee,

Thank you for the touching framed picture of our family. I had tears in my eyes when I saw it! This is the only photo I have of our entire family together, and it means so much to me. You chose an absolutely beautiful frame, too; it looks wonderful in the family room. Please give Uncle Will a big hug for me. I'm looking forward to seeing you both at Thanksgiving. Thank you again, Lee-Lee—I can't tell you how much this means to me.

Love,
Jackie

CASUAL
FOR GIFT AND TIME

Mark,

I just had to sit down and write you a serious thank-you note for the amazing birthday gift you and the guys gave me. I never thought I'd have a set of golf clubs this nice! Also, thanks for coming into town. It meant a lot to have all of my buddies together on my birthday, and it was the perfect day for 18 holes. I had a total blast. Now I've got to figure out what to do for your big 4-0! I hope to see you again really soon. Thanks again for making it one of the best birthdays I've ever had.

Drew

CASUAL
FROM CHILD

Dear Grandma,

Thank you for bringing me the cool markers, crayons, and paints! I had a lot of fun learning how to draw and paint with you. I hope you'll come back and paint with me again really soon. Thanks for being a great grandma!

Love,
Ashley

Dear Mrs. Richter,

We really appreciate the lovely poinsettia you sent to our family for Christmas. It looks beautiful in our front window. It was the first holiday gift we received this year, and it helped us feel like the holidays were really here! We hope that you and Mr. Richter have a wonderful holiday. Thank you for thinking of us in such a festive and thoughtful way.

Happy holidays,
Lisa Elliot

FORMAL
FROM FAMILY

Dear Lauren,

Thank you so much for the beautiful hand-carved soaps you brought over on Saturday. I had no idea fig smelled so good…I think I'm hooked! I couldn't have asked for a better housewarming party, surrounded by all the people I love most in the world. Thank you again for your wonderful gift and even more wonderful friendship.

Sincerely,
Jocelyn

SINCERE
GIFT AND CELEBRATION

Dear Mr. and Mrs. Sexton,

On behalf of Michael and myself, thank you for the pewter candlesticks you gave us for our wedding. They add such an elegant touch to our mantel, and we just love them! Our wedding was a dream day for us both, and the best part was having our dearest friends and family there to celebrate with us. Thank you for helping make it the happiest day of our lives.

Sincerely,
Laurie Wright-McMurray

FORMAL
WEDDING THANK-YOU

sample *thank-you* notes for support & acts of kindness

CASUAL
FOR SUPPORT

Dear Kelly,

Thanks for lunch yesterday. I can't tell you how much our talk helped me put things into perspective. I'm feeling so much better now! There are few things in life as important as good friends, and I'm really lucky to have one as caring as you. Next time, let's get together on a happier note (and let's go ahead and get the cheesecake). Thanks for being such a good friend.

Love,
Karen

CASUAL
FOR HELPING OUT

Dear Steve,

We did it! We're moved, and we simply could not have done it without you.Thanks a million for taking time out of your weekend to help us. I'm sure you had plenty of better things to do than drive that big truck. We really appreciate it. When it comes time for Lisa to move to college, you know you've got your moving crew ready and waiting! Thanks again—now, on to unpacking!

Sincerely,
Lynn and Chen

EMOTIONAL
FOR SUPPORT

Dear Char,

After what's been a very difficult couple of months, I wanted to take a minute to thank you from the bottom of my heart for all the love and support you have given me throughout all of this. My father's illness has been heartbreaking for me—and your stories about your dad have really helped me know what to expect and to prepare myself for what's to come. Having you there to listen to me, encourage me, and lift me up when I've needed it the most has made such a difference on so many different days. Thank you so much, Char.

Your friend,
Emily

Dear Anita and Roger,

We just got back home after an absolutely perfect long weekend at your lake house, and all we can say is…Thank you! Thank you! Thank you! It was so generous of you to let us use it for our special weekend, and we cannot say enough wonderful things about it. The deck was our favorite part—we spent every morning out there reading and relaxing. We're looking forward to dinner together next weekend. Thanks again—you're such great friends.

Fondly,
Eric and Julia

WARM
FOR GENEROSITY

Dear Dr. and Mrs. Bhatia,

Thank you so much for the kind condolence note you sent after Louise's passing. Thank you, too, for the generous contribution you made in her name to the Wellness Foundation. I know that Louise would have been as honored and grateful as I am. Your kind words and warm thoughts helped make a very difficult time easier. Thank you, again, so much.

Sincerely,
Martin Tremblay

WARM
SYMPATHY
ACKNOWLEDGMENT

Dear Tim,

Now that I'm up and around again, I want to thank you for helping me out so much after my knee surgery. From running me to my appointments to making sure I had groceries and clean clothes to wear, you really made my recovery time go smoothly. It was nice to be able to just focus on healing and getting stronger. Now that I'm on my feet again, I hope I can come help you out with your big backyard project. I'll come over this weekend and see how it's going. It's the least I can do to express my thanks to you for being such a great friend.

Talk to you soon!
Mario

HEARTFELT
FOR HELP

sample *thank-you* notes for social events & hospitality

COMPLIMENTARY
TO FRIENDS FOR
DINNER PARTY

Dear Alan and Linda,

Thank you for hosting such an enjoyable dinner at your home on Thursday. The meal was outstanding, and Patrick and I are still dreaming of the chocolate cake! We laughed and replayed jokes and conversations in the car the whole way home. We truly enjoyed your hospitality, and it was so nice meeting Laura and Phil. We always have such fun with you. Thank you again for a fantastic time…let's get together again soon.

Sincerely,
Lynn Murphy

FORMAL
FROM HOSTS TO GUESTS

Dear Mr. and Mrs. Mazur,

On behalf of my wife, Ruth, and myself, I want to thank you for helping us celebrate my retirement in style. We had such a nice time visiting with you both. Thank you, too, for the lovely silver tray. It will make a very nice addition to our dining room. My retirement party is a night we'll always remember. Thank you for being there to celebrate with us.

With gratitude,
Arthur Elrich

CASUAL
FROM GUEST OF HONOR

Dear Kayla,

That party was crazy-fun! Thanks! I can't believe you found a way to get all the girls together and surprise me at the same time. The food, the drinks, the music, everyone there…I couldn't have asked for a better birthday. And we sure did shut the place down, didn't we? Thanks for knowing just what I need, just when I need it. And just you wait until your birthday comes.

Love you,
Viv

Dear Eleanor,

I really appreciate all you did to make me feel so at home this weekend. From your fantastic lasagna to our relaxing afternoon on the patio, your warm hospitality just didn't stop. I know how busy you are, and I really appreciate the time it must have taken to prepare for my visit and tend to my every whim! I'm really looking forward to being able to open my home to you in June! Thanks for such a nice visit.

Gratefully,
Gracie

PS: I hope your tournament goes great this weekend!

WARM
FOR HOSPITALITY

Dear Maria,

I want to take a minute to thank you for having my sister and her kids to your barbecue last weekend. I know you had to scrounge up chairs, extra plates, and everything else, and I want you to know how much it meant to me. They had a great time. In fact, they spent the rest of the weekend talking about it! I'd like to take you to lunch this weekend as my way of saying thanks. I'll give you a call soon to discuss.

Thanks again, Maria!
Eva

CASUAL
TO FRIEND FOR
HELPING OUT

Dear Roger,

Thank you very much for the enjoyable dinner at L'Orient this past Saturday. We truly enjoyed sharing such a fantastic meal with you. We had a five-star evening. Thank you, too, for so generously picking up the tab. We'd very much like to treat you to some of our town's famous seafood when you are here in May. Again, our sincere thanks!

Regards,
Michael and Marianne Muller

PROFESSIONAL
TO FRIENDS FOR
DINNER OUT

contents:

CHAPTER TWO

① ② ③ ④ ⑤ ⑥ ⑦ ⑧

Congratulations

As we know all too well, life can be busy, tough, and just plain draining. So when a good thing happens to someone, it's something to get excited about! And knowing how to write warm, personal congratulatory notes is something to get excited about, too.

So get up on your feet and celebrate good news! Then sit back down with confidence (*and a pen*), because these are happy little notes that feel great to write! And in the process, we get to do a little quality connecting with somebody, which is also a pretty great feeling.

CHAPTER INTRODUCTION

why *congratulatory* notes matter

A really great congratulatory note tells someone you've heard about her big news and are happy for her. It tells her that you care about her, admire her, and are celebrating right along with her. It adds to her joy. In a nutshell, great congratulatory notes make happy people feel even happier. What's not to love about that?

6 parts of a *congratulatory* note

No matter the occasion, great congratulatory notes are made up of the following six parts. All you have to do is add the details!

Dear Denise and John, ①

② *Congratulations, Mom-and Dad-to-be! Your mother shared your happy news with us, and we couldn't be happier for you. You're both so caring and easygoing that you're going to make terrific parents. We can't wait to see everyone when we're in town for Christmas! Until then, our heartfelt congratulations and warm wishes for a healthy pregnancy and a happy Baby Williams.* ③ ③ ④ ⑤

Sincerely, ⑥
Ryan and Sarah Miller

① GREET THE RECIPIENT
② EXPRESS YOUR CONGRATULATIONS
③ REACT TO THE NEWS
④ COMPLIMENT & LOOK AHEAD
⑤ RESTATE YOUR CONGRATULATIONS
⑥ GIVE YOUR REGARDS

great *congratulatory* notes: step by step

① GREET THE RECIPIENT

Your opening line sets the tone for your whole note, so why not start if off right?

- Always use the correct form and spelling of names. Nicknames can be tricky. Not sure if Rodney would like to see "Rod" or "Rodster" in writing? Use discretion—and his full first name.

- Be as formal as your relationship with the recipient. If you're not clearly on a first-name basis, go ahead and use his or her full name with the proper title (*Miss, Ms., Mrs., Mr., Dr., etc.*). If in doubt, remember that too formal always beats too familiar.

② EXPRESS YOUR CONGRATULATIONS

Clearly give your congratulations, as well as a mention of the occasion, in the first sentence of your note.

- Don't be afraid to use upbeat, fun language for close friends and happy occasions: *Congratulations, Mom-and Dad-to-Be!* or *Girl, you did it… Congratulations!*

- When in doubt, or for not-so-close relationships, keep your congratulations straightforward and warm.

③ REACT TO THE NEWS

Let the recipient know what you think about her news—it will convey excitement and sincerity.

- Write briefly about why the occasion is such good news.
- Explain how and when you heard the news, if not from the recipient, and be sure to state your reaction.
- Remember—it's important to verify news you hear "through the grapevine" before sending a note. Avoiding embarrassment for you and your recipient is always a good thing.

④ COMPLIMENT & LOOK AHEAD

Compliment her. After all, good things happen for a reason. Then, look ahead to let her know you will continue to think about her, even after the initial excitement settles.

- Tell her why she deserves her success or happy news.
- Show you know her—write about her talents, past experiences, hard work, or other traits that have helped her get here; or simply say that she is the kind of person worthy of good things.
- For formal notes or for notes to people you do not know well, write about the merit, impressiveness, and importance of the event or occasion.
- Look forward to an upcoming event or the next time you'll see her.
- Express confidence in her future success and offer help or advice if appropriate.
- Not a close relationship? Just say you're thinking about her and wishing her well.

TIMING

The rule of thumb: Send your note as soon as you hear the news, whether it's right away or months after the fact. If you're late finding out, it's perfectly ok to send a note that says so. The recipient will understand and be glad to get your note. Trust us.

⑤ RESTATE YOUR CONGRATULATIONS

Leave the recipient feeling great with an upbeat, complimentary, or very sincere congratulations at the note's end.

- Remind the recipient what the note is all about.
- Express your excitement or compliment again.
- Keep it short and sweet.

⑥ GIVE YOUR REGARDS

Carefully choose a closing appropriate for the recipient.

- "Sincerely" is a good general closing.
- Really excited? Try closing your note with *Hooray!* or *Totally excited for you!* to really convey how happy you are.
- For closer relationships, consider warmer closings such as "Your friend" or "Love."

For a list of great regards for all kinds of occasions, check out the Great Endings section on page 216.

3 MORE THINGS ABOUT CONGRATULATORY NOTES...

Just a few well-chosen words of congratulations can do some heavy lifting—they can amplify happiness, boost a mood, and bolster your relationship.

Good news and happy life events deserve big, enthusiastic recognition. Life's too short to let these kinds of things go by.

Great to write and great to receive... congratulatory notes are real win-win deals.

SECTION NO. 1

congratulatory notes for life events

Think about important occasions for a minute. Births. Weddings. Graduations. Isn't it true that the notes from these important days are the ones people keep and cherish? The reason is pretty simple—events, large and small, are what mark the ages and stages of our lives. And when we congratulate people at these important times, we not only add to their joy…we share it.

So the next time you sit down to write a congratulatory note for someone's important life event, just think, 10, 20, even 50 years down the road, she just might pull your note out of a scrapbook or shoebox and be reminded of one of the happiest times in her life. Now, that's a congratulations with staying power.

REASONS FOR SENDING

Big Life Events

Great notes can help deliver emotional messages for happy milestone events when congratulations are customary, such as:

Graduation

Religious rite of passage (*like baptism, confirmation, bar mitzvah*)

Engagement, wedding, milestone wedding anniversary

Pregnancy, birth, adoption

Retirement

Little Life Events

What a welcome thing a great note would be to help celebrate smaller, more personal, often nontraditional life events, including:

New home (*especially a first home or one in a new city*)

Positive change made (*taking a new path in life, starting a business*)

Major purchase (*car, motorcycle, kitchen remodel*)

New pet

TIMING

Just found out? Send your note as soon as possible. Many of the larger life events also involve a ceremony or party, so consider hand-delivering your note to the event. If you won't be attending or if you prefer to send it, be sure to time it so your note arrives on or around the big day.

4 great *congratulatory* notes for life events

This is a rich, meaningful message of congratulations from one couple to another on the occasion of a long-awaited adoption. Sam and Maria add a lot of warmth by complimenting the cute baby and expressing confidence in Max and Stephanie's parenting ability.

Dear Max and Stephanie,

A heartfelt congratulations on the adoption of your new baby girl. We just received her announcement and picture, and all we can say is "Wow!" A beautiful baby like Laurel is absolutely worth the wait! She is going to be such a blessing and also very blessed. You two will be such wonderful parents. We can't wait to see your new family together at Max's mom's next month! Congratulations, again—we couldn't be happier for you.

Sincerely,
Sam and Maria Lindquist

It seems likely that this note is coming from someone who knows Lewis only a little, perhaps through his parents. But it's still a warm, complimentary note that's made more meaningful by showing some knowledge of Lewis, specifically that he's soon going to college.

Dear Lewis,

Congratulations on your graduation! I was so pleased when I opened your announcement. It hardly seems possible that you could be finished with high school already. However, with your many talents, I know you are more than ready to succeed in college this fall and beyond. I look forward to hearing about the many exciting places life takes you, so please keep in touch. Congratulations and best of luck to you!

Sincerely,
Mrs. Eldon Parker

WORTH NOTING: The sender signs her name Mrs. Eldon Parker. Many married women prefer to be formally addressed like this (Mrs. + husband's name). When Lewis thanks Mrs. Parker for her gift, he will know how to address the envelope.

Dear Gabriela,

Girl, you did it…Congratulations! I was so excited when you told me about closing on the house. You're going to love being a homeowner! With your great style, I can't wait to see what you do with your new place. I'm looking forward to coming over once you get settled. Let me know if you need any help moving things over, OK?

Hoooooooray!
Shel

This casual note between good friends recognizes a pretty big life achievement, becoming a homeowner for the first time! The fact Shel knows Gabriela's move-in date, not to mention her sense of style, suggests a close relationship, but we also see closeness in the informal language, the offer of help moving, and the note's warm and upbeat closing.

Dear Leo,

You're retiring…Congratulations! After all your years of hard work, you've sure earned it! Of course, the best part is now you'll have more time to spend with your baby, the Corvette! I know you're going to have her looking great, and I can't wait to hear all about your cruising and traveling. I hope you can make it back for the summer fishing tournament. My warmest congratulations and wishes to you, Leo.

Your friend,
Gary

Gary makes his note more meaningful by showing real knowledge of his friend. He knows exactly what Leo will want to do with his newfound free time, and he shares in his friend's anticipation and excitement.

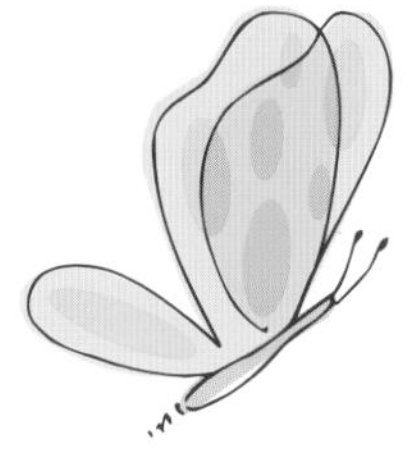

writing your *congratulatory* note

TO GET STARTED, THINK ABOUT THE QUESTIONS BELOW:

Why is this person—and her celebration—important to you?

How did you hear the news? What was your reaction?

What do you think she's feeling right now?

What do you think she'd like to hear the most?

Was this event a long time coming?

Are you confident in the person's abilities? Why?

What admirable qualities got her here? How will they help her in the future?

If you've experienced this life celebration yourself, do you have any tips to offer?

Would you like to offer help in the coming weeks, months?

Will you see this person soon?

FEELING STUMPED?
We've included additional sample notes at the end of this chapter to get your creative juices flowing.

Now, following the steps on pages 56-58, use your answers to the questions—along with the helpful words and phrases we've included on the following pages—to put your congratulations into words!

some of our favorite words for *congratulatory* notes for life events

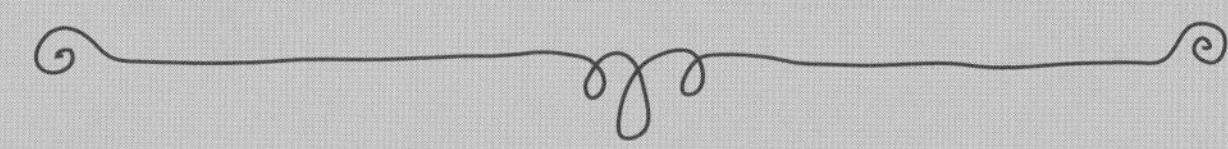

DESCRIBING YOUR CONGRATULATIONS:

Warm	*Heartfelt*	*Hearty*	*Happy*
Special	*Big*	*Earnest*	*Well-Deserved*
Wholehearted	*Deep*	*Sincere*	*Genuine*

DESCRIBING YOUR FEELINGS ABOUT THE NEWS:

Happy	*Thrilled*	*Surprised*	*Touched*
Thankful	*Delighted*	*Overjoyed*	*Moved*
Inspired By	*Tickled*	*Excited*	*Jazzed*

DESCRIBING THE NEWS ITSELF:

Welcome	*Awesome*	*Joyous*	*Super*
Blessed	*Exciting*	*Fantastic*	*Great*
Long-Awaited	*Excellent*	*Wonderful*	*Noteworthy*

a few great phrases for *congratulatory* notes for life events

I'm so (happy) *for you!*

I couldn't be (happier) *for you.*

It couldn't have happened to a (nicer) *person.*

I was so (excited) *when I heard!*

I can only imagine how (proud) *you must be feeling right now.*

What (wonderful) *news!*

I can't wait to (go to your wedding, meet your new baby, see your new home)!

I know you're going to enjoy (parenthood, being retired, your new puppy).

You're so (bright and hardworking)*…you're going to make* (a great nurse).

Thinking of you at this (happy) *time!*

Enjoy every minute of this (special time in your life).

If there's anything at all I can help with, please let me know.

CONGRATULATIONS! YOU'VE WRITTEN ONE HECK OF A GOOD NOTE WHEN...

Someone feels like you're celebrating right along with her.

She feels even more optimistic about the next phase of her life after reading it.

She's going to finish reading your note with a big smile.

SECTION NO. 2

congratulatory notes for achievements

"Well done" isn't just a way to cook a steak. It's the message we want to send to a person who has accomplished something worthy of notice. After all, it takes a lot to get ahead, to stand out from the crowd, to realize our dreams. And when any of those things happen...it's noteworthy. And note-worthy, too!

One of the best things about congratulatory notes is that they can do a lot in just six little steps! They can express our happiness for some-one, recognize hard work and talent, celebrate good news, and look forward to the future! Best of all, they can make people feel even better about what they've achieved. And after writing a great note, we can feel a great sense of accomplishment, too.

REASONS FOR SENDING

Some of the most common kinds of achievements that call for a note include:

New Job

Whether it's a first job or a twentieth, new jobs are both exciting and nerve-wracking! A great note can help someone focus on the positive and feel great!

Promotion

Someone's hard work paid off—let her know how happy you are for her!

Work Anniversary

Spending 5, 10, or 20 years on a job is quite an achievement. Be sure to honor, celebrate, and affirm colleagues, as well as friends and family, on jobs well done!

Awards, Honors, Merit

Find out about the award so you can write knowledgeably about what an impressive achievement it really is!

Sports Achievements

Winning a game, finishing a run, even learning how to ride a bike! These notes can honor and bring a smile.

Personal Goals Realized

Someone ran a 10k race, stopped smoking, learned to ski? People all have personal goals, and when fulfilled, they are achievements worth noting!

Acceptance to a College, University, or Program of Study

With more and more people going back to school later in life, these notes are not just for young people anymore. Whether a high schooler or a grandma, honor the accomplishment of getting accepted and the dedication it takes to tackle the hard work ahead!

TIMING

Send your note as soon as possible after hearing good news. However, if there's a party celebrating the achievement, you might want to hand-deliver your note to the event. If not, just get it there as soon as you can!

4 great *congratulatory* notes for achievements

This is a simple, natural, and warm note of congratulations going to a family member or good friend. Lina recognizes that Marjorie has wished and worked for this achievement, and affirms both Marjorie and her decision while expressing confidence in the future. Bet Marjorie is smiling ear to ear after reading it.

Dear Marjorie,

David just told me you've been accepted into the degree program at the University… Congratulations! I know you've dreamed of doing this for years. I couldn't be happier for you. I am so inspired by your drive and motivation—and you should be proud of all the hard work it took to get yourself here. I know I sure am, Marjorie. Congratulations!

Love,
Lina

WORTH NOTING: Lina tells Marjorie right away how she heard the news.

Patricia's note to her fellow community member is warm and complimentary. She maintains a more formal tone by addressing Ms. Van Hare by her title and last name, but keeps her note friendly by mentioning specifics about Ms. Van Hare's work and the award ceremony. Receiving a note this nice would be an honor in its own right!

Dear Ms. Van Hare,

Please accept my sincere congratulations on receiving this year's community service award. I truly enjoyed attending the ceremony recognizing you and the many different ways you've helped so many people in our area. Your dedication, hard work, and civic-mindedness are an inspiration to us all. Once again, congratulations on this well-deserved honor.

Sincerely,
Patricia Maddox

Dear Aisha,

Heartfelt congratulations to you on your new job—what wonderful news! We were so excited for you when you told us. You have such a heart for teaching, and we know you're really going to make a difference at your new school. They're lucky to have you! Congratulations and best wishes in your new position!

Sincerely,
Richard and Joy

Here's an enthusiastic, affirming note that shows meaningful knowledge of its recipient and her passion for her work. Because Aisha is beginning something new, Richard and Joy close their note nicely with a wish for all the best in her new endeavor.

Dear Barb,

Warmest congratulations on your 20th anniversary with our company. When I read the announcement, I was reminded of your dedication and creativity and of a lot of good memories made through the years. I hope today's celebration will be one such memory for you. Again, my sincere congratulations to you. You're an inspiration to all of us!

Sincerely,
Irv Erickson

It really is an achievement to work somewhere for 20 years, and this note recognizes that accomplishment nicely. Irv's note is both professional and warm, striking a balance between keeping a respectful work-appropriate tone and reflecting shared work experience. Barb is sure to feel honored and grateful.

writing your *congratulatory* note

GET READY TO SUCCEED BY ASKING YOURSELF THESE QUESTIONS:

Why is this person and her achievement important to you?

How did you hear the news? What was your reaction?

What do you think she is feeling right now?

What would she like to hear from you?

Did she work hard for her achievement?

Why is an achievement of this kind important or impressive?

What traits helped her achieve this?

What admirable qualities will serve her well in the future?

Do you have any specific wishes or hopes for her?

Do you have plans to see her in the near future?

PS
Sample notes are always included at the end of every chapter, including this one!

Now that you've answered these questions, you have good information to base your note on. Just follow the steps on pages 56-58 to put it all together. And remember, we've compiled some great words and phrases on the following pages to help steer your note in the right direction.

some of our favorite words for *congratulatory* notes for achievement

DESCRIBING YOUR CONGRATULATIONS:

Warm	*True*	*Hearty*	*Full-Blown*
Enthusiastic	*Sincere*	*Loud*	*Well-Earned*
Heartfelt	*Giant*	*Big*	*Deserved*

DESCRIBING YOUR RESPONSE TO THE NEWS:

Happy	*Touched*	*Proud*	*Moved*
Excited	*Thrilled*	*Gratified*	*Impressed*
Blown-Away	*Psyched*	*Pleased*	*Heartened*

DESCRIBING THE ACHIEVEMENT:

Well-Deserved	*Huge*	*Important*	*Impressive*
Praiseworthy	*Wonderful*	*Prestigious*	*Difficult*
Outstanding	*Rare*	*Inspiring*	*Admirable*

a few great phrases for *congratulatory* notes for achievement

Congratulations to you on (your recent promotion).

What (fantastic) *news!*

Bravo! You really earned it.

It couldn't have happened to a (more deserving) *person.*

There's no one more qualified for the (position) *than you!*

I couldn't be (clapping any louder) *for you.*

I can only imagine how (happy) *you must be.*

You should be proud of (all your hard work).

You're such (a natural leader).

You're going to make (an excellent manager).

This is just the start of many good things to come for you.

I'm looking forward to (watching your career blossom).

YOU SHOULD FEEL PROUD OF YOUR NOTE WHEN...

The recipient feels even more deserving, accomplished, and capable after reading it.

She feels like you really know her and understand her hard work, ability, and talent.

She feels like she just got a big pat on the back!

sample *congratulatory* notes for life events

PERSONAL ACKNOWLEDGEMENT FOR ENGAGEMENT

Dear Diana,

On behalf of George and myself, I congratulate you and Jonathan on your recent engagement. Your sister shared the news this past weekend. How exciting! The two of you are a wonderful couple, and I just know you'll have a wonderful future together. George and I have shared 43 happy years of marriage, and I wish you the same lifelong happiness.

So happy for you both!
Anabelle Krieder

WARM KEEPSAKE NOTE TO BABY FOR BAPTISM

Dear Jackson,

Even though you can't read this yet, I want to congratulate you on your baptism. I'm so glad to be here to share this special day with you. And though you've been with us only for a few months, you've already stolen my heart—and everyone else's, too. I can't wait to watch you grow up! May God bless you and watch over you always, my sweet boy.

I love you!
Grandma Jenny

HEARTFELT WISH FOR WEDDING

Dear Lee,

I want to offer my heartfelt congratulations on your marriage. I'm so happy that you and Tom have found each other. You are a wonderful and inspiring couple. I hope your lives are filled with happiness and love…from this day forward! Congratulations.

Sincerely,
Elaine Lin

Dear Sam,

Congratulations on your bar mitzvah. It's such a happy day for you and for the whole family! We know you've worked very hard to get here, and we're so glad we're able to share it with you. In honor of this important event, we've made a donation to the Foundation in your name. We're very proud of you, and we know you're going to continue to work hard and learn a lot. Mazel Tov!

Love,
Aunt Liz and Uncle Don

AFFIRMING
TO TEEN WITH GIFT

Dear Lloyd and Theresa,

We just wanted to send a quick note, before you left on your trip, to say congratulations on making your lifelong dream come true. Remember back when we'd sit on the deck and you would both talk about spending a summer visiting France one day? Well, that day is here! You both have worked so hard for it, so have a wonderful trip. We can't wait to hear all about it when you get back (if you ever come back!). We're so proud of you both.

Love,
Frank and Norma

SUPPORTIVE
FOR PERSONAL DREAM
REALIZED

Dear Bree,

Just a note to congratulate you on the newest little member of your family…Suzie the Pug! I'll bet the kids are just going crazy for her. She's one lucky little puppy to grow up in a house so full of fun and love. I can't wait to come meet her in person next weekend. Congratulations!

Your willing doggy-sitter (and sister),
Theresa

CASUAL AND SWEET
FOR NEW PET

sample *congratulatory* notes for achievements

BUSINESSLIKE AND COMPLIMENTARY ACKNOWLEDGEMENT

Dear Isaac,

Congratulations on your promotion to project manager! I was so pleased to hear the news this morning. You are well-known around here for your creativity, flexibility, and vision, and I know those fine qualities will serve you well in your new position.

I couldn't be happier for you or for our company—congratulations!

Sincerely,
Marianne Shea

CASUAL AND WARM FOR COLLEGE ACCEPTANCE

Dear Dan,

Just a quick note to say congratulations on getting into Springfield University! Lane just told me the news. And I hear you got the Vance Scholarship, too...Wow! I know what a special award that is and how hard you must have worked to earn it. Guess you got the brains in the family (ha, ha)! But seriously, you're going to love SU—I sure did! If you'd like to chat or even take a road trip up there this summer, I'd love to tell you about it or show you around. Again, congratulations! I'm really happy for you. Talk to you soon.

Your cousin,
Sam

CELEBRATORY WITH GIFT FOR CHILD

Dear Sarah,

I just heard you won the spelling bee at your school—wow! I know how hard you have worked this year at school, and it sure looks like your hard work is paying off. I'm including a gift certificate to the bookstore so you can go pick out something special to celebrate your big win. I can't wait to come visit you next month...until then, know how proud I am of you!

Love you,
Grandma

Lauren!!!

You got the job…Congratulations! I hate to say I told you so, but I knew that it was just a matter of time before they called with the offer. I'm sad you're going to have to relocate but excited I'll have such a great friend in the "big city" now. You're going to take that town by storm! Let's find time next week to go out and celebrate your fantastic news.

So excited for you!
Penelope

UPBEAT
TO CLOSE FRIEND
FOR NEW JOB

Dear Mr. Meyers,

Congratulations on winning the bike tour this weekend! As an avid fan of the sport, I think it's great to see a local athlete take the top prize. And as a dad of Boy Scouts, I also wanted to thank you for the athletic training program you have put in place for our local scout troops. You're a real motivation and inspiration to the boys and to us parents, too. Congratulations again on your win, and best of luck with the race in July!

Sincerely,
Adam Kortoza

COMPLIMENTARY
FOR SPORTS ACHIEVEMENT

Dear Marcia,

Just a quick note to say congratulations on getting your article published! Your dad told me the great news. Ever since you were a little girl, I know you've dreamed of being a writer. How wonderful that you've made your dream come true. I'll be watching my mailbox for the June issue. I just can't wait to read it. Congratulations, Marcia…I'm so proud of you!

Love,
Aunt Lucy

WARM
FOR GOAL REALIZED

contents:

Important Days

Salt and pepper. Peas and carrots. Some things just go together. Important days and putting our feelings into words go together, too. April 10th and Lisa's birthday, Father's Day and Dad, Christmas and the Millers. Important days matter to us because the people we care about matter to us. And whether we choose to send a note or add a warm personal message inside of a greeting card or gift, knowing what to say and how to say it on important days is really something to celebrate!

CHAPTER INTRODUCTION

why notes for *important days* matter

Great notes are one-of-a-kind expressions of our relationships with people. Whether it's on a friend's birthday or on Christmas, when we send someone a note on an important day, we're saying, *One of the things that makes this day important to me is my relationship with you.* Far from obligatory or expected, these kinds of messages really help make an important day even more special. In fact, they're like little one-of-a-kind gifts from us to them.

6 parts of a note for *important days*

Dear Mike, Mary, Claire, and Tony, ①

The leaves are rustling, our turkey's picked out, and all that's left to say is…
② *Happy Thanksgiving! We're wishing you a day filled with good food, good times, and grateful* ③
④ *hearts. We miss you all and sure hope we'll be able to spend next Thanksgiving back home.*
Eat an extra helping of Mary's sweet potatoes for us, and know we're thinking of you all today. ⑤

Lots of love, ⑥
Kristen and Ian

① GREET THE RECIPIENT
② MENTION THE DAY
③ ELABORATE
④ BUILD THE RELATIONSHIP & LOOK AHEAD
⑤ SUMMARIZE
⑥ GIVE YOUR REGARDS

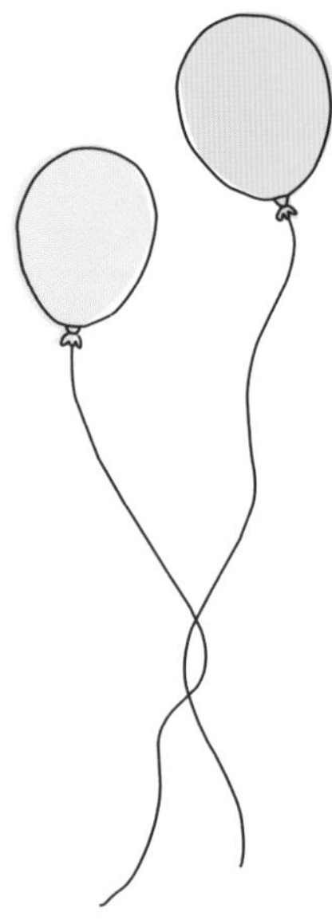

great notes for *important days*: step by step

① GREET THE RECIPIENT

Is this note for one person? A couple? A family?

- Make sure not to leave anyone out.
- Be careful that everyone's name is spelled correctly.

② MENTION THE DAY

Come right out and make it clear why you're writing in the first line of the note—and don't hold back on the enthusiasm!

- Call it her day: *Your special day is here…Happy Birthday!*
- Or get right to the point: *Merry Christmas!*

③ ELABORATE

Write about the person, the significance of the day, as well as what's going on in her life, and don't skimp on the warmth!

- Make wishes for the day and the year ahead.

- Evoke shared holiday experiences, memories, and details.
- Compliment her.
- Show you know her by talking about plans, rituals, or traditions she and her family may have for the day.

④ BUILD THE RELATIONSHIP & LOOK AHEAD

Reaffirm the relationship by looking forward to spending time together or talking soon—or just let her know you're thinking of her on the day.

- Express anticipation for the next time you'll see her, whether it's a holiday or not.
- For close relationships, consider mentioning the meaning of the day and how it relates to your relationship.
- If not a close relationship, look ahead and make a general, simple wish for prosperity and happiness.

TIMING

Because these notes are all about an important day, getting them there on the day itself (or up to three days before) is great. Though a belated note is better than no note at all, be sure to acknowledge your tardiness. People will still be glad to know you thought of them!

⑤ SUMMARIZE

End your note the way it began—with mention of the day and the reason for writing.

- Restate your wishes—consider making a specific wish that shows you know her.
- Use language appropriate for the holiday: *Here's hoping it's the best Mother's Day yet!* or *Joy to you and yours!*

⑥ GIVE YOUR REGARDS

- For close relationships, consider warm regards like *Love, Your loving sister, Hugs and Kisses*, etc.
- These can be fun and festive notes, so consider getting into the spirit by ending with holiday-specific regards like *Ho, Ho, Ho!* or *Your Valentine* or *Boo!*

A complete list of great endings can be found on page 216.

IT'S AN IMPORTANT DAY, BUT DON'T PANIC...

From friends to family to colleagues, we know *a lot* of people. And that adds up to a lot of important days to remember, which can get overwhelming fast. But we've got good news—these kinds of notes are always optional.

Yes, you heard us right. You're not obligated to send a note to every person for every important day, not even for the traditional winter holidays. Write notes for the special days and people that mean the most to you. Write to some people at one holiday and others at another as the occasions and your relationships with the recipients encourage you.

So take a deep breath and repeat after us—*It's my choice. It's up to me. I make the rules.* Try to keep the experience enjoyable for yourself and you'll write better notes! Just wait and see.

SECTION NO. 1

writing notes for people's *special days*

If our hearts had daily planners, certain dates would belong to certain people. We'd have them circled. Double underlined. Exclamation points. Their names written all over them. Capital letters. You get the picture.

After all, these are days that are important to us because they belong to people who are important to us. What better time to sit down and tell them so! And with just a few tips and tricks, you can make your notes for these special days personal and meaningful, which can make special people's special days even better.

REASONS FOR SENDING

Birthdays

Every person who matters to you has one—every single year—which makes these among the most common types of notes you'll send. The great thing is you can also make these among the most personal and meaningful ones you write by focusing on making the recipients feel special, known, and cared about.

"Honoring" Days

People take their roles in life very seriously, and notes sent on special days designated to honor those roles tell people that they are important to us and that we remember them.

Send notes on, for example, Father's Day, Mother's Day, Grandparents Day, Administrative Professionals Day, Cancer Survivors Day, Nurses Day, Veterans Day, or the many other specially designated days, weeks, or months throughout the year that may call specific friends and loved ones to mind.

TIMING

Time your note so that it arrives on the big day or up to three days before. But remember that people are still likely to appreciate a belated note that says nice things about them!

PS: Giving a Card or a Gift?

Adding a personal note is a great way to warm up a greeting card or a gift. Even if you'll see the recipient on her special day, a great note makes your card or gift especially personal and caring. Try including some specific memories, thoughts, or wishes in your note to make her feel like it really is "her" day!

4 great notes for people's *special days*

Rich detail and the power of a very specific memory make this Father's Day note very personal. Also, the memory Ashley shares with her dad leads up to a nice compliment and warm ending.

Dear Daddy,

It's almost Father's Day, and like every year about this time, I've just turned on the AC. I remember an especially hot Father's Day years ago when you played out back with us kids. Then we came inside, and you cranked up the window unit and fed us ice cream until we were all shivering in our shorts and t-shirts! What a good memory…and what a great dad you've always been. I'll be thinking about you on your special day and looking forward to visiting you next month!

Lots of love,
Ashley

This is a very warm birthday message for a beloved niece. Joe and Gladys make their note even more meaningful by tailoring their wishes for Samantha to this time in her life, when she is likely just starting out in a career and setting up her own home. With a note this personal and warm, Samantha is sure to feel like her aunt and uncle really know her and love her.

Dear Samantha,

Happy Birthday, Sweetheart! It's hard to believe it was 25 years ago today that you first came into the world. Time flies, but one thing hasn't changed since then, and that's how much we love you. We hope your birthday will be a time for celebrating all you've accomplished so far…and for looking forward to all you have yet to do! Remember to wish big when you blow out those candles! Happy Birthday!

Love,
Uncle Joe and Aunt Gladys

Dear Sheila,

On Administrative Professionals Day, I want to thank you so much for all you do around here! You not only keep this place running smoothly, but you do it with a great attitude and a lot of caring. Most days you just make it look easy, but today, I hope it really is easy for a change—light day, long lunch, and lots of goodies! I hope you enjoy it all, because someone who does so much for all of us every other day of the year really deserves it! Have a great day.

Sincerely,
Alan

Such a highly complimentary and appreciative note from either her co-worker or a supervisor will make Sheila feel great. By showing awareness of all she does, Alan is building the relationship, a good idea when you need to continue to work well with a person.

Dear Kay,

It's National Cancer Survivors Day, and of course, I couldn't help thinking of you. It's a day of celebration, and I'm celebrating the wonderful attitude and courage you've shown these past four years. You're not just a great friend; you're a real inspiration. I'm so grateful for your friendship and you. As far as I'm concerned, Kay, today is your day!

Love always,
Elyse

It just makes sense to think of a friend who has survived cancer on National Cancer Survivors Day. Elyse takes the thought one step further by writing a note to her friend Kay. National days like this aren't obligatory sending occasions at all, but again, special day notes are best when they're not about obligation, but about people and relationships.

writing your note for someone's *special day*

TO WRITE A NOTE THAT'S FULL OF PERSONAL DETAILS, ASK YOURSELF THESE QUESTIONS ABOUT THE RECIPIENT:

Why is the person important to you?

What qualities or quirks do you admire about her?

What's your favorite memory of her?

What do you wish for her in the next year of her life?

What would her perfect day look like?

What do you think she'd like to hear most today?

What's the significance of this special day?

Will you see her on her big day? If not, when?

Is there a story related to this day or time of year to include?

Is this a difficult day or year for her for any reason?

NEED MORE MOTIVATION? We've included additional sample notes at the end of this chapter.

With the answers to these questions fresh in your mind, follow the outline on pages 84-86 to write your own special note. To jump-start things, great words and phrases are listed on the following pages.

some of our favorite words for people's *special days*

DESCRIBING THE DAY:

Important	*Happy*	*Enjoyable*	*Great*
Memorable	*Best*	*Special*	*Unforgettable*
Relaxing	*Big*	*Fun*	*Perfect*

DESCRIBING THE PERSON:

Appreciated	*Fun*	*Giving*	*Respected*
Sweet	*Fantastic*	*Generous*	*Loved*
One of a Kind	*Funny*	*Dedicated*	*Thoughtful*

DESCRIBING YOU:

Grateful	*Inspired*	*Fortunate*	*Appreciative*
Excited	*Lucky*	*Thrilled*	*Happy*
Celebrating	*Thankful*	*Blessed*	*Honored*

a few great phrases for people's *special days*

It's (Father's Day) *and I couldn't help thinking of you!*

Your (big) *day is here…*(Happy Birthday)*!*

You're on my mind on (Grandparents Day)*!*

On (Nurses Day), *I'd like to take a moment to tell you…*

I hope your day is filled with (relaxing moments).

Today is a day to celebrate (my wonderful sister).

May your day be (unforgettable, one big party)!

I hope you'll find a little time today to (play in your garden)!

Today I'm wishing you (a perfect day for golf)!

I'm so glad I get to celebrate your day with you.

Know I'll be celebrating you all day long today!

Again, have a (wonderful, beautiful, memorable) *day!*

YOUR NOTE IS SOMETHING SPECIAL WHEN...

You wish your recipient a day spent gardening in her yard, and she feels like you really, really know her.

You say so many nice and complimentary things to her that she feels like it truly is her day.

She knows you're thinking of her on her special day and feeling grateful to have her in your life.

SECTION NO. 2

writing notes for *holidays*

Gratitude at Thanksgiving. Love on Valentine's Day. Reflection on New Year's. Certain holidays go hand in hand with certain feelings. And just as different holidays bring with them different emotions, our notes can, too. They can tell the important people in our lives, *You matter to me*, and *I am thinking of you today.*

And though many of us see our holiday cards or newsletters as our once-a-year chance to do some connecting, life offers us many other opportunities throughout the year to do so, often on a smaller, more personal scale. All it takes is a little practice to keep the holiday spirit alive all year long.

REASONS FOR SENDING

Which holidays are important to you and your circle of family and friends? Some might hold special meaning for you or someone you care about, while others might just be your personal favorite. Whatever the reason, holidays big and small make for festive and fun times to send notes. And the only rules for notes of this kind are to be creative and enjoy writing them!

Some commonly celebrated holidays include:

- New Year's Day
- Valentine's Day
- Memorial Day
- Independence Day
- Labor Day
- Halloween
- Thanksgiving
- Winter Holidays *(Christmas, Hanukkah, Kwanzaa)*
- Other Religious Holidays *(Easter, Passover, Diwali, Eid)*

PS: If you write greeting cards for holidays...

While sending cards to those we care about is a time-honored tradition on holidays, the messages we put into them can often be short and impersonal. By using the steps outlined in this chapter, you can add a little extra "happy" to your holiday cards.

TIMING

Time your note or card so that it arrives on the holiday itself or up to three days before. But even if your note arrives a little late, people will be glad you thought of them. A notable exception is during winter holidays. With the volume of mail being sent and received, sending your note any time during the holiday season—which stretches from early December through New Year's Day—is perfectly acceptable.

4 great notes for *holidays*

Mom is sure to appreciate this warm, lighthearted Valentine message from her son. Jamal's note is more powerful than it may seem at first glance, since it recalls a specific memory and takes Mom back to a time that clearly meant a lot to both mother and son. It also makes for a creative and loving way to show Mom that her son is thinking of her.

Dear Mom,

It's Valentine's Day, and I can't help thinking of you—my very first Valentine! Remember how proud I was one year seeing the construction paper card I'd made you displayed on your dresser? You didn't even seem to mind that it was "For a Very Sweat Mom." I hope you know you're just as important to me now as you were then, and I hope you have a happy Valentine's Day this year.

Love you,
Jamal

Shared fall memories make Annabelle's note to her grandparents personal and memorable. Specific details help bring sender and recipients a little closer together at a favorite time of year.

Dear Grandma and Grandpa,

There are pumpkins on all the front porches in our neighborhood, which can mean only one thing…it must be getting close to Halloween! I have so many good memories of playing in the leaves and eating caramel apples at your house, and I want you both to know how much you're in my thoughts this time of year. I also want to share a picture of a pretty cute little pumpkin. Wish we lived closer so Marshall could trick-or-treat at your house! Hope you have a spooky one! Can't wait to see you at Christmas!

Lots of love,
Annabelle

WORTH NOTING: The sender mentions the photo she has enclosed, so her grandparents will be sure to look for it if they don't see it right away.

Dear Stephen and Lynn,

We just wanted to send a quick note to let you know how much we're looking forward to your annual fireworks-watching party. You have the perfect backyard for watching the city display! This summer trip is something we look forward to all year, and we're almost packed! Can't wait to celebrate with you guys this weekend. See you soon!

Fondly,
Ethan and Robin

Ethan and Robin's short-but-sweet preholiday note lets Stephen and Lynn know that they're looking forward to their yearly holiday visit. Quick, warm, upbeat, and friendly, it sets a great tone for the upcoming visit.

Dear Chris, Amy, and Mattie,

Season's greetings from the Zack house to yours! At this happy time of year, we're thinking of you and just how much you mean to us the whole year through. Here's wishing you peace, joy, and lots of memorable family moments this holiday season.

We're looking forward to seeing all of you at the cookie swap!

Fondly,
Tim, Liz, and Emma Zack

This is a purely "holiday" message, with no mention of Christmas, Hanukkah, or any other specific religious occasion. This might be the Zack family's preference, or it might be out of respect for the recipients' beliefs or traditions. Either way, "Seasons Greetings" or "Happy Holidays" are safe ways to go, and they can still be warm, as this note shows.

writing your *holiday* notes

READY TO GET FESTIVE?
THINK ABOUT WHO YOU'RE WRITING YOUR NOTE TO AND ANSWER THE QUESTIONS BELOW:

What is the significance of the holiday?

What kinds of emotions does this holiday evoke?

Why does the recipient come to mind this holiday?

Is there something specific she does on this holiday?

How does she feel about this holiday?

What do you hope her holiday will be like?

Any shared memories of this holiday that would be fun to include?

Is this a difficult or challenging year for her?

Do you know how or with whom she will spend the holiday?

Will you see her on or during the holiday? If not, when?

REMEMBER:
We've included additional sample notes at the end of this chapter.

Now that you've answered these questions, you have more than enough information to write a great note—just follow the steps on pages 84-86. We've listed some great words and phrases for your note on the following pages, too, just in case you need them.

some of our favorite words for *holidays*

DESCRIBING THE DAY:

Festive	*Safe*	*Joyful*	*Romantic*
Enjoyable	*Merry*	*Peaceful*	*Nostalgic*
Fun-Filled	*Perfect*	*Relaxing*	*Meaningful*

HOLIDAY EMOTIONS:

Gratitude	*Joy*	*Love*	*Reflection*
Hopefulness	*Pride*	*Cheer*	*Togetherness*
Thankfulness	*Excitement*	*Romance*	*Comfort*

THINGS WE DO:

Celebrate	*Have Fun*	*Enjoy*	*Share*
Remember	*Gather*	*Visit*	*Count Blessings*
Commemorate	*Relax*	*Party*	*Pray*

a few great phrases for holidays

Even though things are (crazy), *I want to stop and wish you…*

On (Easter), *I'd like to take a moment to tell you…*

It's (Halloween), *and I can't help but think of you!*

You've always known just how to make a holiday special!

Hope your day is (spooky, sweet, happy, merry, fun).

I hope you'll find some time to enjoy (the warm weather).

My (Valentine's Day) *wish for you? That's easy…*

I get a little (nostalgic, baking-obsessed) *this time of year.*

(Thanksgiving) *is about* (gratitude), *and I'm so* (thankful) *for…*

I'm so happy to be sharing this holiday with you.

I'm looking forward to (your 4th of July barbecue)!

Even though you're far away, I'm thinking of you this (Easter).

FOR HOLIDAY NOTES, 3 THINGS MATTER MOST

Details—like mentioning what kinds of decorations are showing up around town (*pumpkins on porches or twinkly lights on every street corner*?), what the weather is like (*is it snowing or is it hot, hot, hot*?) and what kinds of food or fun activities are taking place (*the stores are all open late or the season's first fresh strawberries showed up*) really make your note extra festive.

Details—like what's on your mind at the holiday (*thinking back to years gone by or looking ahead*), what your note's festive theme is (*Peace*? *Reflection*? *Partying*? *Love*?), what wishes you have for the recipient (*a good time with friends or family or health and happiness in the year ahead*?)—make your notes sound warm and uniquely suited for each holiday.

Details about the recipient—like remembering her favorite ice cream flavor, a best-loved gift from years past, a much-loved way to spend a special day, the names of her kids, friends, or pets or her plans for the holiday—lend your note an air of genuine caring and authenticity.

sample notes for people's *special days*

CLOSE & AFFIRMING BIRTHDAY FROM PARENT

Dear Nadia,

Happy birthday! Every year since you've been born, I've made a special wish for you on your day. This year, my wish for you is simple. You don't need luck because you never cease to amaze me with the smart choices you make and the admirable way you handle everything that comes your way. So I'm wishing you a happy, fulfilling year. And remember, today and every day I'm cheering for you, loving you, and so very proud of you.

Love,
Dad

CASUAL & FUNNY BIRTHDAY

Dear Stan,

You made it to 50…Happy Birthday! I hope you have an absolutely perfect day today. You deserve it! I hope you get sun, no wind, and I hope you finally make par! Hey, it's your birthday; anything is possible! But seriously, know I'm thinking of you on your day and wishing you a happy celebration and a great year ahead.

Your much younger brother,
Nick

WARM KEEPSAKE 1ST MOTHER'S DAY

Dear Patrice,

I wanted to be the first to wish you a very happy first Mother's Day. It's been so touching to see what an absolutely wonderful mom you are to Nicole. She's a very lucky little girl who has a lot to celebrate today! I hope you find some time to relax and spoil yourself a little on your special day; no one deserves it more!

Your friend,
Gillian

Dear Julia,

I couldn't let the day go by without wishing you a very happy birthday. You're such a sweet person—I've really enjoyed getting to know you this past year. If next week's not too crazy around here, let's try to get away from the office long enough to go grab lunch together…my treat! Again, happy birthday! I hope you have an absolutely perfect day!

Sincerely,
Gloria

COMPLIMENTARY BIRTHDAY WISH WITH INVITATION

Dear Mr. Dobson,

On Veterans Day, I want to thank you so much for all you've done—and continue to do—for our country. From your honorable military service years ago to your passionate community leadership today, you're a great example and inspiration to all of us. I look forward to watching our city continue to benefit from your involvement and perspective. Happy Veterans Day.

Warmly,
Elliot Grainger

HONORING VETERANS DAY

Dear Marion,

Happy Birthday to the best wife and mother in the world! Forget worrying about laundry, soccer practice, or anything else. It's time to focus on you. Enclosed is a gift certificate to the Bliss Spa so you can enjoy some well-deserved pampering next Saturday. I'll handle everything at home while you're there. You do so much for me and the kids all year long. I hope your day is just great!

I love you,
Andrew

WARM & APPRECIATIVE BIRTHDAY TO WIFE WITH GIFT

sample notes for *holidays*

FESTIVE MISS-YOU HOLIDAY

Dear Patty and Paul,

The halls are decked, the cookies are baked, and now it's time for the fun part—sending warm wishes to great friends like you! We sure do wish you lived closer and could just drop by. We miss your bright smiles and wonderful company and are really looking forward to seeing you in the coming year. The happiest of holidays to you both!

Your friends,
Lorraine and Gil

FUNNY BETWEEN FRIENDS ON VALENTINE'S DAY

Piper…

Happy Valentine's Day…NOT! I hope you spend the day NOT eating chocolate, NOT getting flowers, and NOT having a romantic dinner out. As for me, I'm thinking some wine, carryout, and a NOT romantic novel will be my festivities of choice. With everyone else in the world getting all mushy—we non-Valentine-loving girls have to stick together! Hope all's well where you are—I miss you!

XOXOXO,
Lexy

NOSTALGIC BETWEEN SISTERS

Dear Christine,

Thanksgiving is all about gratitude, and I couldn't let it go by without letting you know how grateful I am to have you for a sister. We have so many traditions and memories shared between us—I think of you a hundred times every holiday. So today, know I'm thinking of you with a thankful heart. And no matter how far away you are, there's always room for you at my table. And no, it's not the kids' table, anymore!

Love,
Agnes

Dear Brahim and Najat,

Finally! Eid is here! We wish you a very happy holiday. It would be great if we were closer so we could all celebrate the day together and share some of Najat's famous cooking! Even though you're across the country, know that we will be holding you and your family in our thoughts and our prayers on this special day. Eid Mubarak!

Blessings and love,
Hamid and Fatima

CELEBRATORY & WARM
EID

Dear Amanda and Joel,

At this special time of year, we thank you so much for all of the hard work and dedication you've brought to our association all year long. It's been a great year, and it's all because of the hard work of dedicated volunteers like you! We hope you have a relaxing, safe, and very happy holiday, and we look forward to another great year of working together. Thank you again for all you do.

Season's Greetings!
Rich and Barbara Kingsman

FORMAL & APPRECIATIVE
HOLIDAY

Dear Michael and Brandon,

Your grandma wanted me to wish you both a very happy Easter and thank you for being such good boys this spring! She says you're playing nicely, saying "thank you," and even keeping your rooms clean. Wow! I hope you like the little goodies I've hidden in your backyard. Your grandma told me what you liked the best. I hope you have a fun time hunting for them and a really happy Easter!

Your friend,
The Easter Bunny

PS: Your grandma wanted me to tell you she loves you very much!

FUN HOLIDAY
TO KIDS

contents:

Love and Romance

Passionate, tender, bittersweet, short, long, steamy, affectionate, sweet, romantic, poetic, apologetic…

Just like there are all kinds of loves, there are all kinds of love notes. And while love notes can be as individual as fingerprints, great ones all communicate the same basic message…eight little letters…three little words…*I love you.*

It's really amazing what great love notes can do. We might think our feelings are understood, and often they are, but sometimes it's not only nice to hear them, it's nice to read them, too. Just wait and see what a world of difference those three little words will make to the one you love.

CHAPTER INTRODUCTION

why *love* notes matter

Though it might not sound very romantic, the truth is that we need to provide our relationships with regular care to keep them running smoothly. That's what love notes are—they're love maintenance. They help keep fun, playfulness, and passion alive, both on special days when they're more expected and on regular days when they come as sweet surprises. They tell the ones we love that they matter to us, that our lives are better because of them, and that we're willing to take the time to sit down and tell them so.

6 parts of a *love* note

① *Dear Adam,*

② *Surprise—I just wanted to add a little sunshine to your day! I know it's been a hard couple of weeks for you at work, and I just wanted to tell you that I think it's really amazing how you always manage to do so much for the kids and me no matter what else is going on your life. You're a remarkable man, a fantastic father, and the best husband a woman could ever ask for. I love you very much. See you at home tonight!* ③ ③ ④ ⑤

⑥ *Yours always,*

Jeannie

① GREET YOUR LOVE

② TELL HIM WHY YOU'RE WRITING

③ AFFIRM HIM

④ NURTURE YOUR CONNECTION

⑤ REITERATE WHY YOU'RE WRITING

⑥ GIVE YOUR LOVING REGARDS

great *love* notes: step by step

① GREET YOUR LOVE

Wow him by making the opening of your note personal.

- Consider using a term of endearment instead of his name.
- Call him yours, *My darling Lou,* or *My sweet Aaron.*
- Use a pet name if you're confident he'll like it.

② TELL HIM WHY YOU'RE WRITING

You want your love to know just what this note is for, so make it clear in this important first line. It can set the tone for the whole note.

- It might be *On our anniversary*...but *I just felt like*...is also a perfectly good reason for a love note.
- If something specific prompted the note, let him know what.
- Tell him what's on your mind, how you're feeling, what's going on.
- Consider using storytelling or *picture this*...approaches to get his attention, and then elaborate on the scene you've set in the next step of your note.

③ AFFIRM HIM
Talk about him! Let him know that you notice and appreciate him and what he does.

- Compliment him or mention his effect on you.
- Comment on what's going on in his life and talk about it.
- Mentioning details about something he's said or done will show him that it really matters to you.

④ NURTURE YOUR CONNECTION
Use this step as your chance to say things you might not every day.

- Mention the importance of the relationship to you—today and tomorrow.
- Express gratitude for the relationship and for him.
- Mention shared jokes and experiences.
- Share anticipation about an upcoming event, large or small, fancy or simple, that you'll be sharing together and tell him why you're excited.

TIMING
Send your beloved a note whenever the mood strikes! For special days, remember that a wise person will get a love note to his or her love on the special day.

⑤ REITERATE WHY YOU'RE WRITING

Make sure your note's end delivers a consistent, clear message.

- Show you know him well by making a wish or delivering a message that suits his tastes and interests.
- Just because—it's nice to hear the note came for no reason other than to make him smile! Let him know that!
- End the note with something to get him excited, whether it's seeing him that night or champagne waiting at home.
- Using those three little words, *I love you*, at your note's end is a good bet every time.

⑥ GIVE YOUR LOVING REGARDS

Love note closings are plentiful—just make sure your closing matches the tone of your note!

- How about: *Love, All my love, Forever yours, Tenderly, Passionately, Gratefully, Affectionately, XOXOXO, Your loving wife, The luckiest woman in the world*...just to name a few!
- Get creative! Consider using pet names or a suggestive, sexy, or sweet closing to make your note really unforgettable!

For a complete list of closings, see "Great Endings" on page 216.

BET YOU'LL LOVE TO KNOW...

You don't have to be a Shakespeare or Browning to write a great love note. Just be your honest, in-love self.

You don't need an occasion to write. Some of the nicest love notes to receive are the ones that come on an ordinary day, for no special reason.

If you feel silly writing your note, just remember how happy your love will be to receive it!

a few notes about *love* notes

NEW LOVE OR LASTING LOVE?

The length of a relationship is a big factor in deciding what to write in a love note. Here are some things to keep in mind for brand-new loves and tried-and-true ones, too.

Considerations for New Love

There are few things more exciting than falling in love, and it's good to communicate that feeling in a note. But try not to come on too strong. Words and phrases like "forever," "always," or "till the end of time" might be inappropriate for a new relationship. Also, it's probably wiser to say *I love you* in person before writing it in a note.

Considerations for Lasting Love

When you've been in a relationship with someone for years, you have a lot of shared experiences to draw on when writing a love note. Tough times allow you to express "Our love is stronger for what we've been through together," while good times make fun messages of gratitude for the person and the relationship appropriate. Even better, shared experiences allow you to use a kind of shorthand. You can say, "Remember that night we camped out under the stars in Colorado? Or…I'm thinking about a weekend at Laguna Beach," and he'll know exactly what you mean.

LOVE AND EVERYTHING ELSE...

People in love, you're also in luck, because the kinds of notes discussed in the other chapters of this book can be adapted for love relationships by including some of the words, phrases, and ideas found in this chapter.

Love notes are unique, because, unlike many other kinds of notes, they can do double duty. Even when an occasion or event calls for a note, love can also be a big part of the message.

Extra Words of Love

Consider the difference between *Happy Birthday!* and *Happy Birthday, Gorgeous!* Even if it doesn't feel natural to use any of the terms listed below, remember that your partner's name can work as a term of endearment if you add it to a loving, complimentary statement like *My handsome Lou* or *My sweet Aaron*.

Baby	Cutie	Honey
My Forever Love	My Friend	My Partner
My Soulmate	(My) Angel	(My) Darling
(My) Dear	(My) Love	(My) Sweet
Sugar	Sweet Girl	Sweetheart
Sweetie	Amazing	Beautiful
Breathtaking	Fabulous	Fantastic
Good-Looking	Gorgeous	Handsome
Hardworking	Kind	Romantic
Sexy	Sweet	Thoughtful

EXTRAS FOR LOVE NOTES

Consider having your note include or accompany a little something special.

- Quote a line or two from "your song"—or any love song that has good, happy, or romantic associations for the two of you.
- Include a quote from a favorite love poem.
- Add a light touch of scent (*consider your perfume or an essential oil*).
- Enclose tickets (*for a movie, concert, weekend getaway, or any other fun date*).
- Have your note accompany a gift (*flowers, chocolate, wine, or any other indulgence you know your love enjoys*).

SECTION NO. 1

love notes for special days

In the real-life fairy tale that is love, even when we're busy living our happily-ever-afters, not all days are created equal. Some special days, like anniversaries, birthdays, or holidays, can be made even more meaningful by really connecting and celebrating with our princes or princesses...and great love notes do just that.

Love notes let the ones we love know that the day is special because they—and our relationships—are special. So, next time there's a special day to celebrate, remember how a love note can add a little extra happy, merry, surprise, and "aww." No magic wand required.

REASONS FOR SENDING

Consider how a love note could help make the following kinds of days even more special.

Anniversaries

Days that have special significance for your relationship call for great love notes. Consider notes to commemorate: Wedding Anniversary, Engagement Date, First Date, Birth or Adoption of a Child, Personal or Shared Achievement

Important Days

What's the holiday all about? Use a day's meaning and emotion as the basis of your loving message.

- Traditional "love" holidays like Valentine's Day focus on romance and love.
- Thanksgiving, Christmas, or the other winter holidays are traditional times to express gratitude, shared religious beliefs, and to look ahead.
- Father's Day and Mother's Day celebrate the important roles of parents and celebrate the special qualities individuals have.
- Birthdays are all about the person—what makes him special and what's wished for him on the day and in the year ahead.

Make Up Your Own Holidays!

What's more romantic than finding out-of-the-ordinary reasons to celebrate with your love? Ideas include: Full Moon, First Day of Summer, Daylight Savings Time, Sports Home Openers, TV Finales, Movie Premieres, and More! Just be creative and have fun!

Don't Forget Difficult Days

A note of loving support on difficult days can make a world of difference. Consider sending a note on the anniversary of the death of a loved one, as well as on holidays following a death or any other rough time in your love's life.

TIMING

These notes should be received on the day itself. Deliver the note in person, leave it in a place your love will find it, or consider mailing it just for fun. You might also wish to write more than one note and time them so that your love receives or finds them throughout the day.

4 great *love* notes for special days

Anna's note offers a lot of recognition and affirmation. By mentioning specifics that mean a lot to her and the kids, her note is especially appropriate for an occasion like Father's Day when she wants to honor Paul AND say "I love you." She also hints at some tough times she and Paul have weathered and references shared dreams and history, all of which lend a very genuine tone to her message.

Dear Paul,

On Father's Day I want you to know how very glad I am to be raising our kids with you. You are an unbelievable father, Honey. This year alone, you have made such a difference to Jonah by helping him make the baseball team and to Claire by starting your father-daughter breakfast ritual and really helping her gain confidence with her math skills. It makes me so happy that we've stuck together all these years and have the kind of family we dreamed about so long ago. Life's not perfect, but there's no one I'd rather be sharing it with than you. Our kids and I are very blessed and lucky to have you. I love you, Paul, more than ever…Happy Father's Day!

Yours truly,
Anna

Sam's note is in no way mushy, yet it still manages to be endearing. He lets Lily know that she is very important to him—past, present, and future.

Dear Lily,

Happy Valentine's Day! Today is a day dedicated to love and, naturally, I can't help but think of you. You've made the past year so happy for me, Lil. It's hard to imagine my life without you in it now. I'm counting on many more Valentine's Days together, and I'm looking forward to our date tonight. Until then, I'm thinking of you with love, sweet girl.

Your Valentine,
Sam

WORTH NOTING: The sender warms his note up with terms of endearment—using Lily's nickname early in the note and "sweet girl" in the last sentence.

Dear Kim,

Today is the anniversary of the day that the most wonderful woman I've ever met was born! So it's a pretty special day for me. And since that day, I can't imagine anyone's come into this world with such a unique blend of beauty, brains, humor, grace, and kindness. I'm one lucky guy! Get your pretty self ready for some steak-n-cake, birthday girl… I'll pick you up at 7.

I love you with all my heart. The celebrating has just begun…

Adoringly yours,
Michael

What a creative—and complimentary—way of saying "Happy Birthday." Lots of people might be sending Kim cards on her big day, but only Michael could give her a note like this. Rest assured she'll remember it for many birthdays to come.

Dearest Jim,

Can it really be five years since we moved into our house? I remember seeing it for the first time together. You looked at me, I looked at you, and we just knew. Today, I want you to know that sharing it with you is what makes it my dream home. So here's to our love and to dreams come true. I'll have the champagne chilled and ready for us when you get home…

All my love,
Janet

Janet's love note to Jim is sent for a different sort of anniversary. It celebrates the shared achievement of moving into their home and recognizes in a very warm way that Jim and the relationship he and Janet share are what make it a dream home for her.

writing your *love* note

"HOW DO I LOVE THEE...UM..." TRY STARTING WITH THESE QUESTIONS:

What's the special day, and why is it meaningful?

What do you think your love would like to hear most on this day?

If a holiday, are there any specific themes that relate to your relationship? For example—Thanksgiving (*gratitude*), New Year's (*Turning over a new leaf*).

What are some of your love's most admirable qualities?

Was there a recent occurrence or event that demonstrated those qualities?

What does your love do to keep your relationship going strong?

What does it mean to have him in your life?

What reasons do you have to be grateful to him and for him?

What are you looking forward to with him?

Can you think of a memory or story your love would like to hear?

NEED MORE INSPIRATION? We've included additional sample notes at the end of this chapter.

Use your answers to these questions and follow the steps on pages 112-114 to create your unique love note. Helpful words and phrases are available on the following pages.

some of our favorite words of *love* for special days

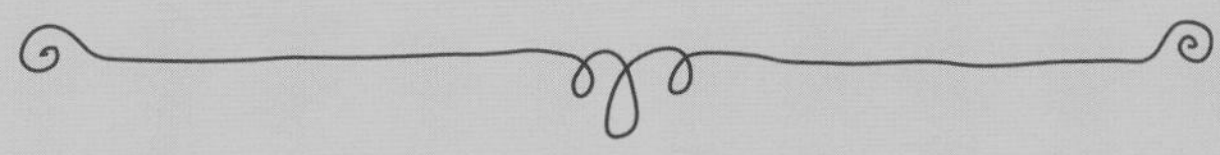

DESCRIBING YOU:

Charmed	*Blissful*	*Lucky*	*Thankful*
Spellbound	*Glad*	*Star-Struck*	*In Love*
Committed	*Blessed*	*Happy*	*Amazed*

DESCRIBING THE ONE YOU LOVE:

Thoughtful	*Kind*	*Handsome*	*Unique*
Admirable	*Giving*	*Fun*	*Beautiful*
Dependable	*Talented*	*Devoted*	*Steady*

DESCRIBING THE DAY:

Important	*Sweet*	*Momentous*	*Long-Awaited*
Unforgettable	*Special*	*Meaningful*	*Enjoyable*
Romantic	*Memorable*	*Lasting*	*Relaxing*

a few great phrases of *love* for special days

On (our anniversary), *I want to make sure you know….*

This is just a note to say, (Merry Christmas)…*I love you.*

Can it really be (22) *years since we* (first met)*?*

I love you (very much, with all my heart, more than you know).

Even though I forget to say it sometimes, I love you.

Now that we're (parents), *you're more* (beautiful) *to me than ever.*

I have so much to celebrate today because….

You're still the one (who gives me butterflies).

Being with you means (I get to spend every day with my best friend).

I have a little (birthday) *surprise planned for you.*

Can't wait to (see you, celebrate with you).

I'm looking forward to (our little getaway, many more wonderful years).

YOUR LOVE NOTE'S A KEEPER WHEN...

The one you love feels like you're celebrating not only the day, but him, too.

He is eagerly awaiting the next time he gets to hug you, spend time with you, have dinner with you.

He is even more secure about the connection you share and your future together.

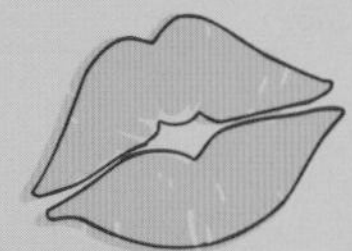

SECTION NO. 2

love notes for regular days

Sexy.

Ok, now that we've got your attention...There are new loves and lasting loves, happy relationships and troubled ones, joined-at-the-hip couples and those loving long-distance. While each love is different, great love notes all say the same basic things...*You are someone special. You matter to me. I love you.*

And who needs a "reason" to write them, anyway? After all, regular days happen a lot more often than special ones, and the best love notes are often the ones that catch us by surprise. So get busy! And remember, the more notes we write, the more kinds we get to try. Wink, wink.

REASONS FOR SENDING

Every day offers the chance to send a little love. Consider the following reasons:

- To say, "Hey, I'm thinking of you today."
- To acknowledge a difficult time for the relationship or for the one you love.
- To say you miss him when he's away.
- To say thanks for the date, for the gift, for being him, for the…well, use your imagination.
- Just because you love him and want to say so.

PS: Your love note will come as an extra-sweet surprise when it's…

Slipped into his briefcase, portfolio, day planner, or gym bag.

Sent to a hotel or packed into his suitcase when he is away.

Tucked into the pocket of his coat, jacket, or pants.

Sitting on the seat of his car or taped to his windshield.

Stuck into his lunch or slipped under his dinner plate.

Mailed to the office or addressed to him at home.

Waiting for him in the fridge or propped against the coffee maker.

Slipped under his pillow or waiting for him on the couch.

Taped to the bathroom mirror…or written in lipstick.

TIMING

The basic idea is to make sure your partner will receive the note at a time when it will really help him, touch his heart, or catch him by surprise. For "miss you" and difficult times, events will dictate the timing. For everything else—it's up to you!

4 great *love* notes for regular days

Wow! Imagine opening your briefcase and finding this note. There's no special reason for it, other than June's epiphany about not expressing appreciation often enough. Writing seems to help her compliment her husband with warmth and thoroughness that aren't always possible in everyday conversation.

Dear Lou,

Just wanted to take a minute to tell you how much I love you. It occurred to me last night that I don't tell you nearly enough that I appreciate you and enjoy sharing life with you. You're funny, sweet, smart, and such a kind and generous husband to me. And I didn't want another day to go by without telling you how much all of those qualities—and you—mean to me. I love you with all of my heart, Lou. I can't wait to see you at home tonight.

Your lucky wife,
June

This thank-you note shows that Will clearly wants to continue to get to know Emma. His real purpose seems to be letting her know he cares about her as a person and about continuing to see her. He helps himself out by not coming on too strong and by remembering how important her work is to her. Emma will surely be surprised—and thrilled—to get such a complimentary note.

Dear Emma,

I want to thank you again for a wonderful date on Thursday. I had such a good time talking with you over dinner and watching your face light up every time you mentioned the kids you work with. You're such a sweet and easygoing person—I'm really looking forward to getting to know you more. Can't wait to see you for our dinner and movie date on Saturday!

Fondly,
Will

Dear Maria,

I wish I could have stowed away in this suitcase (or this envelope!) so I could be there with you now as you read this note. You've been gone only a short while, but already I miss your beautiful face, sweet smile, and the sound of your voice ringing through the house. While you're away, remember—there's someone back home missing you, loving you, and counting the days until you're back in his arms.

I love you,
Gerald

A lot of physical details in this love note make it appropriate for a "miss you" message. Gerald imagines Maria reading the note, compliments features he misses seeing and hearing, and expresses a desire to have her "back in his arms." This approach gives both of them something nice to hold on to while they're apart.

Dear Jerry,

Although our whole family is hurting right now, I wanted to take a second to tell you how much I'm thinking of you in particular. We both loved your dad, but I know how hard losing him hit you. I want you to know I'm here for you, Honey. I'm always here to talk, reminisce, sit together, or just get out of the house and take a walk. I'm thinking of you and loving you more than ever.

Yours always,
LeeAnn

We expect sympathy notes from friends and colleagues, but not necessarily from our spouses. And if you think about it, it's the person closest to us that often knows just what to say to make us feel better. This double-duty love/sympathy note does a great job of that—achieving a nice balance of loving affection and caring support at a difficult time.

writing your *love* note

OK...NOW FOCUS, FEEL THE LOVE, AND ASK YOURSELF THE FOLLOWING QUESTIONS:

Why are you writing? A great date? A rough time? Just because?

Close your eyes and think of the one you love...What do you see?

What are his most admirable qualities?

How do you feel when you're together?

Is there anything you feel but don't express very often?

What special things does he do for you? For your family? For others?

What does it mean to have him in your life?

What do you think your love will be doing when he reads the note?

Is he away? What do you miss the most?

Is your loved one—or your relationship—going through a difficult time?

Are you confident that things will get better?

What are you looking forward to doing together?

REMEMBER:
We've included additional sample notes at the end of this chapter.

Now, following the steps on page 112-114, use your answers—along with the words and phrases on the following pages—to help your love note sing.

some of our favorite words of *love* for regular days

DESCRIBING YOU:

Head Over Heels	*Dazzled*	*So Happy*	*Passionate*
Smitten	*Content*	*Glad*	*Undeserving*
Thrilled	*Emotional*	*Grateful*	*Fortunate*

DESCRIBING THE ONE YOU LOVE:

Wonderful	*Irresistible*	*Adorable*	*Heavenly*
Kissable	*Sweet*	*Generous*	*Sexy*
Funny	*Cuddly*	*Lovable*	*Good-Natured*

DESCRIBING THE RELATIONSHIP:

Exciting	*Special*	*Blissful*	*Amazing*
Comfortable	*Fun*	*Lasting*	*Romantic*
Passionate	*Unique*	*Gratifying*	*Strong*

a few great phrases of *love* for regular days

Just felt like writing a note to say…

I love you more than (anyone else in the whole world).

Even though I don't say it nearly enough, (I'm so happy to have you).

I'm so glad (fate, life, God) *brought us together.*

You do so much to (take good care of our family).

I love the way you (scoop me in your arms when you get home).

I'm so grateful for (what we have together).

You've been gone only (a day), *and I miss you already.*

I'm looking forward to (our weekend in the city).

I want you to know I'm always here for you.

I'm thinking of you all day long today.

Remember, there's someone who (loves you with all her heart).

YOUR NOTE WILL TURN A REGULAR DAY INTO SOMETHING SPECIAL WHEN...

The one you love knows, without a doubt, how you feel about him.

He feels great knowing you find his smile so sexy or all the things he does for you so amazing.

He puts down the note and thinks, *Wow. I'm one lucky guy!*

sample *love* notes for special days

WARM & HEARTFELT
WEDDING ANNIVERSARY

Dear Frank,

Twenty-nine years—can you believe it? It seems like yesterday that we were standing in that church surrounded by our friends and family. It was one of the happiest days of my life. The years we've shared since have certainly had their ups and downs, but the one constant through all of it has been you and your love. Your strength, your generosity, your selflessness, and your commitment to our family have never wavered. And I feel like I have more to celebrate every single year…thanks to you. So, happy anniversary! I love you.

Yours,
Anita

SWEET
OWN SPECIAL HOLIDAY

Dear Louise,

Happy first day of spring! You know what that means? Tonight we'll open our first bottle of Pinot Grigio at home on the deck and celebrate making it through another long, cold winter together. And still, there's no one in the world I'd rather snuggle with when it's cold and celebrate with when it's warm than you. This makes Spring Celebration No. 9 for us, and we just keep getting better year after year.

Cin-cin,
Jay

SUPPORTIVE
ANNIVERSARY OF
DEATH OF SIBLING

Dear Mitch,

I know today is a tough day for you and one that you've replayed over and over for 11 years. Ron would have turned 50 this year, and I know you'll be thinking of him and how much you love and miss him. So today, I want you to know, I'll be sending you my love, support, and good thoughts all day long. I know I can't make it any easier, but I want you to know my love is always with you.

Hugs and kisses,
Amy

SENTIMENTAL
NEW YEAR

Dear James,

Here it is, the last day of the year, and I'm a little sad to see it end. After all, this was the year we got married. And while I simply cannot wait to keep realizing all the dreams we've built together in the new year, I'm going to pause at 11:59 and say a great big thanks to you and to the universe for making this past year the happiest of my life. So here's to auld lang syne, and here's to you. I love you with all my heart.

Sappy as ever,
Kate

NOSTALGIC
SPECIAL ANNIVERSARY

My Dear Patrick,

While you're driving home, I want you to remember something for me…18 years ago, at just about 6 P.M., I was on my way to McConnel's Grill to meet you for the first time. Little did I know that night, but I was about to meet the man who would fill the next 18 years of my life with laughter, kindness, generosity, and love. Thank you for 18 great years, Honey. I can't wait for the next 18! I have some special plans for us tonight…starting when you get home. I love you and can't wait to see you. Drive safely.

Yours always,
Eileen

CONGRATULATORY
ADOPTION ANNIVERSARY

Dear Sarah,

Can you believe we've been parents for a whole year now? It seems like just yesterday that we brought Jake home. We sure have gotten through a lot this year…two flu bouts, chicken pox, some falls, and even allergies. And although it's really Jake's day, I want to take a minute to celebrate you. Jake's really lucky to have such a caring, kind, and generous mother. And I'm lucky to have the same person as my partner in parenting and in life. I love you!

Always,
Craig

sample *love* notes for regular days

SWEET AND
COMPLIMENTARY
JUST BECAUSE

My Sweet Teri,

Although it's just a regular day, I want to tell you three very important things that are on my mind today…You're beautiful in every way. I feel so lucky to be married to you. I love you more than ever.

Baby, I can hardly wait for our cruise next week. It's going to be so good to spend some time alone together. Until then, remember, I love you…I love you…I love you.

Forever yours,
John

SURPRISE WITH GIFT
MISS YOU

Dear George,

Surprise! Right now, you're probably just reaching in your bag for your magazines. I hope these cookies will be a sweet little reminder of home while you're away. I know this is a big trip for you—and I know you're going to do a great job. I think I'm probably the proudest (and luckiest) wife in the whole world. I'll be thinking of you and rooting for you the whole time you're gone. Have a safe trip, Honey. I'll talk to you tonight.

All my love,
Mary

IMAGINATIVE
THINKING OF YOU

Good Morning, Sweetie,

I can picture you right now…sitting at your desk, opening up your laptop and smiling when you see this note tucked inside. I can also see the little dimple at the corner of your lip as you smile at these words. Now I want you to picture me…staring out my office window thinking of your beautiful face, looking at that picture of us in Mexico at least a hundred times a day. And even though I know I'll get to hug you, kiss you, laugh with you, and talk with you tonight at home, you'll still be on my mind all day today.

Fondly, madly, truly,
Todd

Dear Scarlett,

Once upon a time, I met a woman. She was kind; she was better than me at poker, but somehow I didn't even mind. She laughed with her whole body, and when she smiled—which was a lot—I couldn't help but feel like the luckiest man in the world. This woman was a wonderful partner, a patient and giving mother, and someone who did so much for everyone around her. One day I realized she'd probably like to know all these things. So I sat down, wrote her a love note, and told her so. And we lived very happily ever after.

Yours,
Vince

ROMANTIC STORYTELLING
JUST BECAUSE

Dear Michael,

When I pulled up to the house yesterday after work, I had to sit in the car for a minute and stare because I couldn't get over how GREAT the house looks! And it hit me just how much work you've done this summer. I guess sometimes I take it for granted that you're up early on the weekends or out in the yard after work—and I know how much of it you do for me. So I want to thank you now for all of the hard work, pride, and love you put into making our house a beautiful home. You're a wonderful husband…and I'm one lucky lady.

I love you!
Patrice

LOVING & AFFIRMING
WITH GRATITUDE

Dear Gil,

Thank you so much for my beautiful bezel-set birthday necklace. And, OK, diamonds really are a girl's best friend. Well, second best…after you! But seriously, Baby, even after all this time, you somehow manage to just keep wowing me. Every single time I wear my necklace—which is going to be a lot!—I'm going to think of the man who loves me like crazy every single day and who knows how to spoil me like no one else can. You're amazing—and you amaze me more and more every year. I love you so much, Gil. Thank you for being you.

Yours always,
Jen

CASUAL BUT WARM
THANKS FOR GIFT

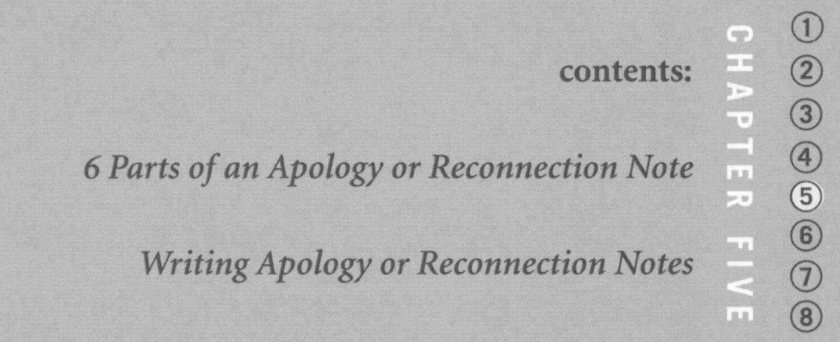

Apology and Reconnection

As different as the two topics may seem, apologizing and reconnecting have some very important things in common. They both mean taking the initiative. They both mean going out on a limb. They both mean reaching out to someone. And, very often, they are both pretty hard things to do.

But we have some good news for you! Knowing a few handy tips and tricks can help you get started down the apologizing and reconnecting road. And once you've written a great note and gotten everything off your chest, you'll feel a lot better...we just know it.

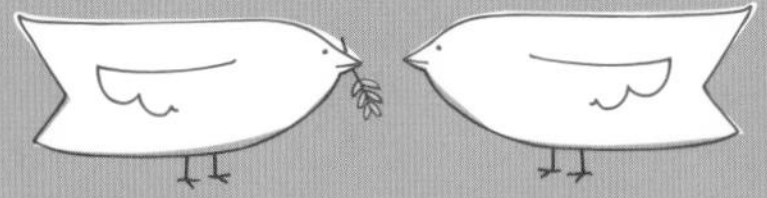

CHAPTER INTRODUCTION

why *apology & reconnection* notes matter

There's a broad range of seriousness—and potential messiness—in apologies and reconnections, but a great note lets you express regret for what's happened and accept blame if and when it's due. A great note can also help clear up any misunderstandings and help both parties move from awkwardness and anger to communication and forgiveness, which feels a whole lot better than silence!

6 parts of an *apology & reconnection* note

It's true—apologizing is tough stuff. So take a deep breath, follow the 6 steps listed in the next few pages, and count with us as you go—1, 2, 3, 4, 5, 6. Before you know it, you'll be finished and feeling a lot better!

Dear Gail, ①

I'd like to apologize from the bottom of my heart for snapping at you this weekend. ② *I really overreacted* ③ *to your comment about Steve, and I know I hurt your feelings.* ③ *I should have kept my cool, and I'm sorry. Our friendship is a whole lot more important to me than my behavior must have led you to believe.* ④ *I'd really love it if we could grab lunch on Wednesday, my treat. I'll call you, ok?* ④ *Again, I'm so sorry, Gail.* ⑤

Your friend, ⑥

Ginny

① GREET THE RECIPIENT

② APOLOGIZE OR STATE DESIRE TO RECONNECT

③ ELABORATE

④ BUILD THE RELATIONSHIP & LOOK AHEAD

⑤ RESTATE APOLOGY OR DESIRE TO RECONNECT

⑥ GIVE YOUR REGARDS

great *apology & reconnection* notes: step by step

① GREET THE RECIPIENT
Get your note off on the right foot.

- Make sure you spell the name correctly.
- Consider upbeat openers like *Hello, Brian!* or simply *Brian!*
- For notes with a more serious purpose, stick with the traditional "Dear Brian," opening.
- For reconnection, try to double check that last names have not changed.

② APOLOGIZE OR STATE DESIRE TO RECONNECT
Check your ego at the door and come right out and say it.

- Say you're sorry for misunderstandings, even if they might not be your fault.
- Take clear responsibility if you were in the wrong.
- For reconnection, express regret that you lost touch, and show a desire to start communicating or to meet.

③ ELABORATE

Focus on the other person.

- For apologies, put her feelings first and address how she must be feeling or must have felt.
- Communicate her importance to you—after all, she needs to know that you think the relationship is more important than the problem.
- For reconnection, compliment her or express interest in her. Help her understand why you want to get back in touch.

④ BUILD THE RELATIONSHIP & LOOK AHEAD

Let her know she matters to you and you'd like to talk or get together.

- Make the first move for a specific time or place.
- If you're nervous about being perceived as pushy, consider including your business card or e-mail address, and give her the opportunity to take the next step.

TIMING

The sooner, the better. That holds true whether you goofed up ten minutes ago or ten years ago. For minor gaffes, try to send your note within three days...a week at most. If it takes you longer, it's good to apologize for both the mess-up and the overdue apology. And take our word for it, when it comes to righting a wrong, better late than never.

⑤ RESTATE APOLOGY OR DESIRE TO RECONNECT

Briefly restate that you're sorry or that you hope to get back in touch.

⑥ GIVE YOUR REGARDS

Use your regards to support your overall message.

- For apologies, consider using the note's closing to reiterate the relationship, *Your Friend, Your Sister.*
- A funny apology? For minor apologies, consider using self-deprecating light humor such as *Your (forgetful) friend* or *Ms. Foot-in-Mouth.* Just be sure your recipient will appreciate this approach!
- For reconnection, anticipate the recipient's reaction. If you think she will be OK with it, try closings like *Your long lost roommate* or *Your neighbor in 4B always.* If you're uncertain of her reaction, keep the closing simple and straightforward with *Sincerely* or your full name.

A complete list of Great Endings can be found on page 216.

A NOTE ABOUT APOLOGIES AND RECONNECTIONS...

"To err is human; to forgive divine." Unfortunately, the people we write notes to are just as human as we are. We can't make them get back in touch or forgive us. We can only ask. We can extend an olive branch. We can put ourselves out there. We can give it a good try. But at some point, after getting no response or an undesirable response, we also have to be realistic, chalk it up to bad timing or misfortune, and move on the best we can.

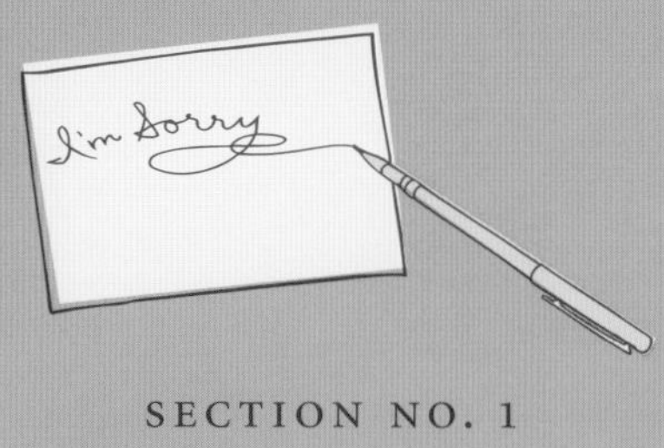

SECTION NO. 1

writing *apology & reconnection* notes

No doubt about it, apologizing or getting back in touch with someone after a long time is often an exercise in courage and humility, if not just plain ego-swallowing. But as hard as these kinds of notes may be to write, they are important. In fact, the possibility that our relationship with another person could be permanently at stake makes the whole apologizing and reconnecting business much more important...but not necessarily easier to do. That's where we come in. If you're ready to suck it up, put it out there, and get it over with...read on.

Oh, go on...you'll thank us later.

REASONS FOR SENDING

Simple Apologies

A short and sweet apology note is appropriate for relatively small things, such as:

- Being late, not showing up, canceling or confusing plans.
- Sticking your foot in your mouth.
- Fighting with a friend or loved one.
- A minor indiscretion, bad behavior, or a simple misunderstanding.
- Failing to follow through on a promise, meet a deadline, etc.
- Declining a social invitation or having to cancel at the last minute.

Complex Apologies Involving Reconnection

Situations that have the added dimensions of time or very bad feelings require notes that are typically meatier than simple apologies. Consider them for situations like a major indiscretion, betrayal, bad behavior, a misunderstanding, or not speaking to a friend or family member for a long time (*from weeks to years*).

Reconnection

People don't always lose touch with one another because of a disagreement, but sometimes just because of a change in circumstances or the passage of time. And the people we remember and want to get back in touch with can vary as much as the circumstances—from someone you used to see daily and now see only rarely to someone you knew years ago who seemed to just disappear off the map.

Some of the most common reconnection needs include former friends and loves, former colleagues or classmates, former neighbors, and relatives you've lost track of.

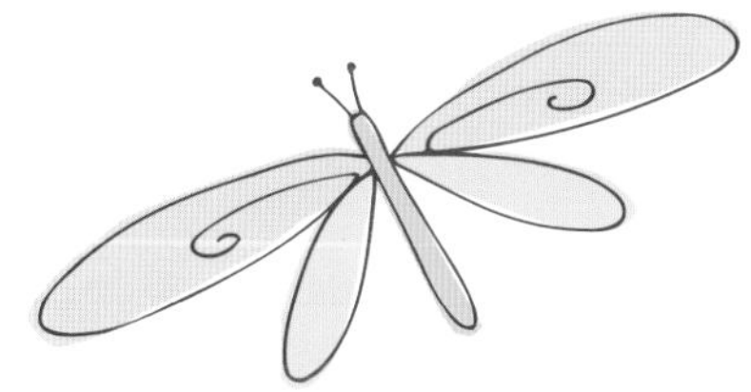

4 great *apology & reconnection* notes

Danielle pulls her foot out of her mouth with a nice measure of humility. It sounds like Bev wasn't particularly offended, but with two relationships at stake (*Danielle's and her child's*), the sender is taking no chances.

Dear Bev,

Please accept my sincere apology for my awful comment about your new work schedule. I realized how petty it was as soon as I left your place the other night. You are absolutely committed to your work, and I was just feeling jealous because I'd like to work out something similar with my job and haven't been able to.

You were very gracious about it, but it was wrong of me, and I'm so sorry. I hope that we—and our kids—can still be friends.

Sincerely,
Danielle

Amy's apology is complicated by time and hard feelings. It seems likely that both sisters are a little bit at fault, but the sender graciously shoulders the blame. She sends the message that the most important thing to her is having her sister back. Warm phrases such as "I love you" and "I miss you" show the once-close nature of their relationship. Amy also makes a specific offer to talk at a designated time and place, which may help facilitate a reconnection.

Dear Edie,

I don't want any more time to go by without telling you how very sorry I am for not speaking to you for so long. I can see now that the problem was never you. It was my being judgmental…and stubborn. I hope that you can find it in your heart to forgive me for the terrible things I said. You're my sister, and I love you…I miss you, too.

It would be really wonderful if we could talk at the reunion next month. I'd love the chance tell you in person how deeply sorry I am. I hope to see you there. Again, I'm so sorry.

Your sister,
Amy

Dear Jodi,

You know, I've really dropped the ball on keeping in touch since Ty was born! I promised myself I'd never lose touch with you, but I realize I have. We used to have such good times, and I'd love it if we could start getting together again. I'm planning to call you this weekend to see what's new with you. (I promise I won't talk about diapers or playgroup…much!) It's been too long—and I just can't wait to catch up!

Your friend,
Meredith

The sender does a good job of expressing interest in her old friend—important for reconnection. Humor is appropriate, because there aren't really bad feelings on either side. The two friends just suddenly found themselves at different life stages and lost touch.

Dear Mark and Dee,

Unfortunately, due to a last-minute change in plans, we will be unable to attend your anniversary party on April 26th as we thought we would be able to. We are sorry to miss it, but we were already committed to attend our niece's wedding in Atlanta that weekend and have just been asked by her parents to come down early to help them with some last-minute arrangements.

Once again, our sincere regrets. We wish you a very happy celebration, and we hope to see you soon!

Sincerely,
Eddie and Vi Campbell

This simple apology note expresses regret for being unable to follow through on accepting an invitation for a social engagement. It's short, sweet, and gracious.

WORTH NOTING: Notes declining invitations to social events are one of the simplest and, perhaps, most often needed forms of apology. They can also be rather uncomfortable to write. Our tip—just be honest, to-the-point, and sincere.

writing your *apology & reconnection* note

READY TO TAKE THAT INITIATIVE?
GO OUT ON THAT LIMB?
START BY ANSWERING THESE QUESTIONS:

Why is the relationship important to you?

Do you miss seeing or talking with the other person?

Why do you want to write this note?

Is there a memory or story you could share to break the ice?

What are you apologizing for? Be as clear as you can.

Why do you regret what happened or losing touch?

Can you imagine what the recipient is feeling and needs to hear?

Does she have a right to be upset, angry, disappointed?

Would you like to talk or get together?

Would you like her to write back or call you?

NEED MORE MOTIVATION?
We've included additional sample notes at the end of this chapter.

Now, use your answers to the questions, as well as some of the great words and phrases on the following pages, and follow the outline on pages 142-144. Before you know it, you'll have a great note of your own.

some of our favorite words for apology & reconnection notes

DESCRIBING YOUR APOLOGY OR WISH TO RECONNECT:

Sincere	*Important*	*Overdue*	*Genuine*
Wholehearted	*True*	*Honest*	*Difficult*
Heartfelt	*Fervent*	*Surprising*	*Belated*

DESCRIBING YOU:

In the Wrong	*Hurtful*	*Unkind*	*Eager*
Overbearing	*Impolite*	*Ungrounded*	*Hopeful*
Inconsiderate	*Insensitive*	*Regretful*	*Excited to (See You, Catch Up)*
Thoughtless	*Stubborn*	*Nervous*	
Antagonistic	*Dense*	*Enthusiastic*	*(So, Very, Deeply, Truly) Sorry*
At Fault	*Upsetting*	*Inspired To*	
Self-Centered	*Rude*	*Optimistic*	

a few great phrases for *apology & reconnection* notes

It was so wrong of me to…

Please accept my apology for…

I really regret (having lost touch with you).

I don't want another day to pass without (saying I'm sorry).

I'm truly sorry for (my awful behavior).

I didn't mean to (hurt your feelings).

You have every right to be (upset with me).

I apologize for not being able to make it to (your shower).

I don't know why we lost touch. I wish we hadn't.

It must seem out of the blue, but (I saw you in the paper).

I hope we can get together (when I'm in town next month).

I know it's been a long time, but I'd really like to (chat).

WHO WOULDN'T WANT TO FORGIVE AND FORGET WHEN...

Your note makes her feel valued and believe her feelings and the relationship are important to you.

She feels empowered to forgive, to move on, or to agree to future contact.

She's hopeful and looking forward to talking, meeting, or hearing from you again.

sample notes for *apology & reconnection*

SIMPLE & SINCERE
APOLOGY FOR MIX-UP

Dear Hannah,

I am so sorry about the mix-up over our movie date. I'm not sure how my signals got crossed, but it's sure too bad that I was at the restaurant waiting for you while you were at the theater waiting for me. I was really looking forward to seeing you again. I hope we can reschedule. I'll give you a call this week to see if you would like to try again this weekend. This time, I'll pick you up!

Jack

HEARTFELT
APOLOGY FOR
"FOOT IN MOUTH"

Dear Alicia,

I owe you a sincere apology for telling the family about the new baby you and Dan are expecting. That was a surprise that should have been yours, and you have every right to be upset with me. I really don't know what I was thinking, and I hope you'll be able to forgive me. I'm looking forward to being there for you during the pregnancy. Again, I'm truly sorry.

Sincerely,
Lisa

FORMAL & PROFESSIONAL
DECLINING INVITATION

Dear Dr. Logan,

I was so honored to receive an invitation to your inaugural address and reception at this year's conference. Unfortunately, I have to decline your generous invitation because my family and I will be out of town that week. I'm so sorry that I am unable to attend. I have been impressed by the important innovations you have made in the field this year and would have truly enjoyed hearing you speak. I know that your address will be a real highlight of the conference. I wish you all the best and thank you again for the kind invitation.

Sincerely,
Andrea Holloway

Dear Brenda,

Let me just say right off the bat that this apology is long overdue. I'm sorry about what I said when we were out with everyone last month. I'm sure you were really embarrassed. It was wrong of me, and I didn't mean it. You're a great person, and I always enjoy being around you. I hope you can forgive me, because I look forward to seeing you again soon. Again, I'm deeply sorry.

Sincerely,
Joan

OVERDUE BUT SINCERE APOLOGY FOR SOCIAL INCIDENT

Dear Chuck,

When I came across the wonderful article about you in the recent alumni magazine, I suddenly realized how much I regret having lost touch with you since college. You were always such a great guy to talk to, and I would love to hear more about what you're up to these days. I'm going to be traveling to Chicago on business this summer (July 13-19), and if we could get together, I'd really like that.

Again, it would be great to hear from you!

Sincerely,
Keith Henderson

WARM & FRIENDLY LONG-TIME RECONNECTION

Dear Dana,

How are you doing? More and more these days I've been thinking what a shame it is that the two of us haven't figured out a way to get together, now that we work at different places. I really miss the laughs we used to have. I was also thinking The Joe Shack is about halfway between your place and mine. What would you think about meeting there for coffee on Saturday morning? I'll give you a call to see if that works for you. Who knows? If it sounds good, maybe we could make it a regular thing…I sure do miss our chats!

Your long lost colleague,
Missy

CASUAL & UPBEAT RECONNECTION

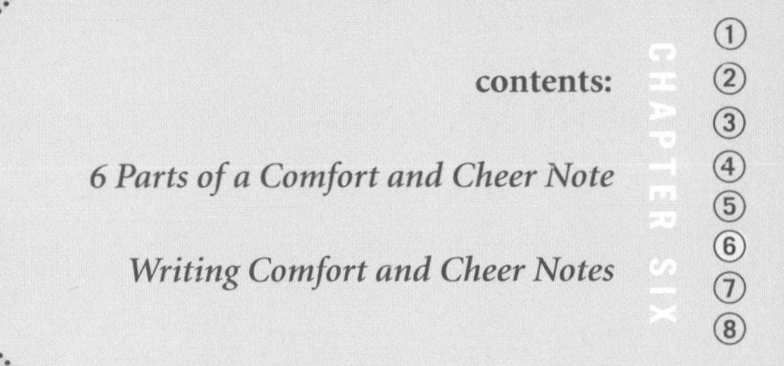

Comfort and Cheer

When someone we know is upset, sick, feeling down, or having a rough time, of course we feel bad for him or her. We truly do care. But if we don't communicate those feelings, either out of fear of saying the wrong thing or because we're "too busy," we can inadvertently send the message that we don't care all that much.

That's where great notes come in. By sitting down and writing a caring note—even if it's short and sweet—we send much-needed comfort and cheer to people we care about when they need it. Far from sending the wrong message, we send a very simple, but much-appreciated one: *I care about you.*

CHAPTER INTRODUCTION

why comfort & cheer notes matter

While the reasons for sending comfort and cheer notes can range from minor to major troubles, great notes have one thing in common—they reach out to their recipients and express caring and support. In just a few little lines, they say: *You matter to me. I care about you. You're not alone.* Little notes sure can do a big job, don't you think?

6 parts of a *comfort & cheer* note

While the situations that call for comfort and cheer notes vary, the basic steps of such notes are the same. It's the details and personality that you add that make your notes one-of-a-kind and personal. Ready to get started? Just follow the steps below.

Dear Dave, ①

We're both thinking of you ② *as you recuperate from your hip surgery. We know it's been a hard couple of weeks for you.* ③ *Knowing you, you'll want to get out there right away, but we hope you'll take the time to relax and spoil yourself a little* ③ *while you heal. We can't wait to come and visit you* ④ *when you get back home.*

Until then, take good care, and know we're thinking of you! ⑤

Sincerely, ⑥

Roger and Gertie

① GREET THE RECIPIENT

② TELL WHY YOU'RE WRITING

③ ELABORATE

④ BUILD THE RELATIONSHIP & OFFER SUPPORT

⑤ RESTATE CARING

⑥ GIVE YOUR REGARDS

great *comfort & cheer* notes: step by step

① GREET THE RECIPIENT

Start your note off right!

- Double-check that you get the spelling of her name right.
- If anyone else's name is mentioned in the note, do the same.
- For close relationships, consider using a pet name or nickname. It could be just the shot of sunshine she needs.

② TELL HER WHY YOU'RE WRITING

Sometimes when someone is having a tough time, it's hard for her to focus, so be straightforward and make sure your message is easy to understand.

- If you're comfortable using unpleasant words in your note like "divorce" or "sick," go ahead and do so. If not, let your recipient know you're thinking of her at her "difficult time." She'll know what you mean.
- Let her know how you heard the news, if not from her.
- Communicate caring by saying you're sorry or that you're thinking of her.
- If she just seems down, and you don't know what's wrong, don't pry. Just let her know you're thinking of her and hoping that things are OK.

③ ELABORATE

Remember, focus on the person, not the trouble.

- Make your caring more personal by adding meaningful details where you can. Mention something your recipient has done in the past, something you've heard about her, something she enjoys doing—anything to set a warm, safe, and friendly tone for the rest of the note.
- Compliment her.
- Show you know her by writing about something specific—her work, a hobby, or a character trait.
- Make a wish for her comfort or recovery.
- Express confidence in her, if appropriate.

TIMING

Do your best to send your note within a week of hearing about the trouble. But remember that even a belated note will do the recipient good.

④ BUILD THE RELATIONSHIP & OFFER SUPPORT

Let her know you understand her need for support, and be specific about how you'd like to help.

- Make yourself available for assistance—physical or emotional.
- Look forward to seeing or visiting her.
- Recall a time when she helped you, and offer to return the favor.

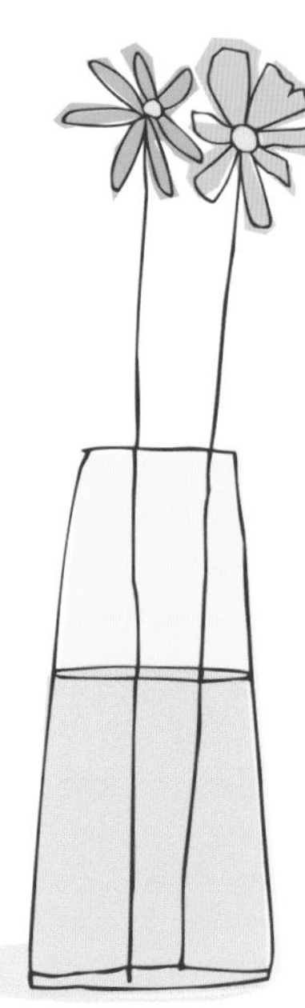

⑤ RESTATE CARING

Briefly remind your recipient that you're thinking of her and wishing good things for her.

- Sum up your note's main point—*You're on my mind, Thinking of you,* or *Know I'll be thinking of you and hoping things get better soon.* These phrases really end your note in a comforting, caring way.
- If you're going to see her soon, reiterate that you're looking forward to it with phrases like *Can't wait to see you!* or *See you soon!*

⑥ GIVE YOUR REGARDS

Base your regards on the level of formality in your relationship and the mood of the recipient.

- For warm relationships, consider *Yours, Your friend, Always, With love.*
- For more general situations, *Sincerely, Thinking of you,* and *Best wishes* are good choices.

Remember, we have a full list of regards for you to choose from on page 216.

SUPER-SIZE YOUR COMFORT AND CHEER...

Here are two of our favorite ways to send an extra dose of comfort and cheer along with your note.

Jot an inspirational quote, a humorous or comforting phrase, or a Bible verse in your note.
A good quote will stick with your recipient and bounce around her head when she needs it most. Just be sensitive to your recipient. Be sure it's something she would appreciate and that it's appropriate for her situation. And take care to quote and attribute it correctly.

Consider sending small gifts
If she's on the mend, emotionally or physically, ideal gifts are those that will help her enjoy herself, relax, or get her mind off what's going on for a bit. Consider sending reading materials, pampering products, music, photos, videos, or treats. Another great option is a gift card to a favorite restaurant, salon, bookstore, or shop. Sometimes indulgence really is the best medicine!

SECTION NO. 1

writing *comfort & cheer* notes

Imagine for a minute that you're having a difficult time. You feel sad. Alone. Upset. Down in the dumps. Pretty darned lousy. Now imagine that someone takes time out of her day to remind you that you are not alone, that people really do care. And, if only for a minute, you feel an amazing thing…hope. It's like that person just pointed up to the sky and showed you the tiniest sliver of silver lining in the clouds above your head. Then you know there's more to life than the hurt you're feeling. That's the power of reaching out. That's what a really great note can do. Ready to make a difference to someone? OK, let's get going…

some of our favorite words of comfort & cheer

YOUR WISHES FOR THE RECIPIENT:

Good Spirits	*Comfort*	*Hope*	*Peace (of Mind)*
Speedy Recovery	*Rest*	*Strength*	*Perspective*
Contentment	*Healing*	*Relaxation*	*Time (to Recover or Adjust)*

WORDS DESCRIBING THE RECIPIENT:

Strong or Tough	*Resilient*	*Positive*	*Courageous*
Big-Hearted	*Adaptable*	*Persistent*	*Kind*
High-Spirited	*Patient*	*Amazing*	*Loving*

WORDS DESCRIBING THE SITUATION:

Frustrating	*Trying*	*Hurtful*	*Painful*
Demanding	*Difficult*	*Challenging*	*Complicated*
Overwhelming	*Intense*	*Confusing*	*Disheartening*

a few great phrases of *comfort & cheer*

I'm deeply sorry to hear that (your sister is ill).

I just heard about (your accident), *and I'm thinking of you.*

I'm wishing you (comfort) *during this difficult time.*

My heart goes out to you.

I hope you're (taking it easy).

You've been so (brave)*…I really admire your* (courage).

I'm praying you'll have (strength) *when you need it most.*

(Our love and support) *are always here for you.*

We can't wait to see you doing the things you enjoy again!

The weeks ahead will be challenging, and I want to help.

Can I (bring dinner over on Thursday night)?*

Let's (have coffee). *I'll call in a few days to set up a time.**

**Be sure to follow through on anything you offer or promise.*

YOUR COMFORT AND CHEER IS REALLY COMING THROUGH WHEN...

Your recipient knows you're thinking of her.

She chuckles even though laughing makes her stitches hurt.

She's comforted and feels hopeful.

sample notes for *comfort & cheer*

LIGHTHEARTED
MINOR SURGERY

Hey Big Guy!

I wanted to wish you a speedy recovery from your foot surgery. It's just not the same around here without you! For one thing, nobody else knows how to make your 'road tar coffee.' Seriously, though, I hope you're resting well and getting around all right. If it's OK, I'd like to stop by Thursday after work, but I'll call before I leave. (Maybe you could give me some coffee pointers!)

Looking forward to seeing you soon!

Sincerely,
Chen

SUPPORTIVE
FEELING DOWN

Hey Landon,

I just wanted to send a little note to let you know you're on my mind. I've noticed you seem down lately, and I've been thinking about you. The last thing I want to do is intrude, but please know I'm here for you in any way I can be. In fact, I'm going to be home watching the game Thursday night. If you want to come hang out, that'd be great. If not, no big deal. Either way, let's catch up soon!

Your friend,
Lottie

SUPPORTIVE
MATERIAL LOSS

Dear Vicki and Al,

Lorraine recently told us about the fire at your lake house—we had no idea and were so sorry to hear the news. I know how much you love going up there, and I hope that you're soon able to get it fixed up better than ever. If there is anything we can do to help out, please know we're here for you. We even have photos of the house from last summer, if those would come in handy! Again, we're so sorry to hear about your loss, and we're thinking of you both.

Sincerely,
Ruth and Rich

Dear Bill,

I read in the Sunday paper that Bergman's closed its office here in town, and I couldn't help but think of you. It was always so clear how much the company meant to you. But what was even clearer than that over your years of impressive work was your talent, work ethic, and amazing resilience. I know you'll be out there again in no time. When things calm down for you, let's go grab a bite to eat together. I'll give you a call this week to figure out a good time.

Until then, you're in my thoughts.

Sincerely,
Mike Jones

COMPLIMENTARY
LOSS OF JOB

Dear Cassie,

I just heard from Melanie about your diagnosis, and I wanted to drop a quick note your way. I know it's been a hard couple of months for you, and your strength and positive attitude have been just amazing. Please know that I'll be thinking of you and hoping that your treatment goes smoothly. I also want you to know that I'm here for you—to talk, visit, or give you a hand with things around the house anytime. I'll give you a call over the weekend to see what might be helpful. Until then, you'll be on my mind.

Love You!
Kylie

WARM
SERIOUS DIAGNOSIS

Serena,

Hi, there, New Momma! I just wanted to let you know how much I enjoyed talking with you this past weekend. I also want you to know I'm thinking about you as you adjust to life with that sweet baby boy. I know what a hormonal, sleep-deprived time this is, but I also know what a tough cookie you are. You're going to have the whole mom thing down in no time. I'm really looking forward to coming to visit next week. And I'm coming to H-E-L-P... so be thinking about where I could help you out most. I can't wait to see you both!

Lots of love,
Paige

CASUAL
NEW BABY STRESS

contents:

Sympathy

What on earth do I say? This thought almost always passes through our minds with events as difficult as death. Sympathy notes might just be the hardest kinds of notes to write, but as hard as they are to write, sympathy notes are some of the most important notes people will ever receive. These notes matter...a lot.

And we're here to help make this daunting task more manageable. So maybe the best thing to do is just take a deep breath before starting and remind ourselves that we're doing something important for someone. And we should feel good about the chance to send a little comfort and caring.

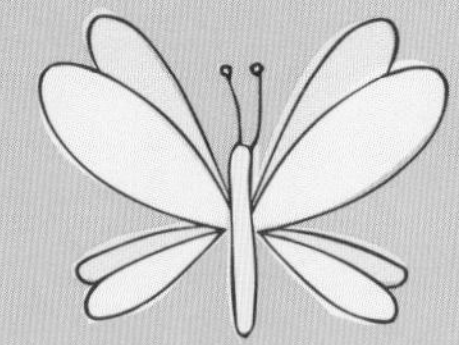

CHAPTER INTRODUCTION

why *sympathy* notes matter

When a death happens, grieving people and families often feel overwhelmed and alone in their pain. They need to be reminded that others care about them. Sympathy notes provide reassurance and comfort by sharing good memories, letting the grieving know we're thinking of them, and often, by making a specific offer of help. The simple gesture of sending a sympathy note is an expression of support and caring that can help ease a grieving person's pain by reaching out and saying, *You are not alone.*

6 parts of a *sympathy* note

Difficult tasks are often made a little easier by breaking them down into smaller steps. By following the steps outlined in the next few pages, you will put into place all six important parts of a sympathy note, and your difficult task will be done. And done well.

Dear Marjorie, ①

I am so sorry to hear that Patty died. She was such a creative and amazing person. I know so many will miss her sweet smile and contagious laugh. My heart really goes out to you. If there is a day that we could go have coffee and talk, I would love to do that. I'll call next week to see if there's a good time for you. ② ③ ④

Again, you have my deepest sympathy. ⑤

Sincerely, ⑥
Jeannie

① GREET THE RECIPIENT
② EXPRESS YOUR SYMPATHY
③ ELABORATE
④ BUILD THE RELATIONSHIP & OFFER SUPPORT
⑤ RESTATE SYMPATHY
⑥ GIVE YOUR REGARDS

great *sympathy* notes: step by step

① GREET THE RECIPIENT

Though it's always important to get your note off to a good start, there are some special considerations for sympathy.

- If you knew the deceased, but not his or her family, address your note to the closest relative—the spouse, parent(s), or oldest child.
- Add "and Family" if you know multiple members of the family.
- Be sure that the names of your recipients and the name of the deceased are spelled correctly.

② EXPRESS YOUR SYMPATHY

Be straightforward and use clear language to aid a reader who is probably very distracted.

- "Died" is not a dirty word. If you're comfortable writing it, do so. For a softer approach, consider using passing, loss, or death.
- It is perfectly acceptable to write a note on behalf of your spouse, family, or colleagues.
- Stick with more formal language for sympathy notes, even if the person is someone you know well. Follow-up notes can be more casual.

- For sympathy follow-up notes—which are thinking-of-you notes that can be sent for a year or more after a death—mention why the recipient is on your mind. If it's a special time of year or date, acknowledge it.

③ ELABORATE

Mention what made the deceased special and memorable to you. Focus on the person, not the death.

- Include the deceased's good qualities.
- Share a pleasant memory.
- If you didn't know the deceased, consider acknowledging their importance to the recipient.
- For sympathy follow-up notes that mark a difficult time of year, anniversary, or date, recall what made this day or time of year special.

④ BUILD THE RELATIONSHIP & OFFER SUPPORT

Let the recipient know you understand her need for support, and be specific about how you'd like to help.

- If you'd like to call or visit, give an idea of when that will be.
- Take the initiative to get together or offer support, but understand that your invitations might not be accepted right away.

TIMING

Send sympathy notes as soon as you hear the news. Even if it's well past the death, the recipient will always be glad to hear from you. Sympathy follow-up notes should be sent as often as you feel comfortable for a year or more following the death. Remember—these are just guidelines. Use your relationship as your ultimate guide to what feels right.

⑤ RESTATE SYMPATHY

- Briefly restate why you're writing.
- Offer sympathy directly at the close of the note.
- Letting the recipients know you're thinking about them is also a great way to end the note.

⑥ GIVE YOUR REGARDS

- General regards such as *Sincerely* are always appropriate.
- Consider *Fondly, Your Friend,* or *Love* for close relationships.
- As long as it isn't redundant, consider an occasion-specific closing like *With sympathy* or *With deepest sympathy.*

Additional regards can be found in the Great Endings section on page 216.

THREE TIPS YOU'LL BE GLAD YOU READ

1. **Keep sympathy notes fairly short**. Your recipient probably has a lot of notes to read and a shorter attention span than she would normally have. So be compassionate, but get right to the point. The quality of your caring is more important than the quantity of your words.

2. **Inspirational quotes, Bible verses, or short poems** are a great way to add a little ray of hope or extra comfort to a sympathy note. These quotes often say something that can be a starting point for your message or just add extra emotion and meaning. However, if you're going to use one, be sure you quote and attribute it correctly.

3. It's OK to **include a lighthearted memory** of, or funny story about, the deceased—especially when it honors the kind of person he or she was. As long as it's something you'd feel OK mentioning in polite company, your recipient will probably appreciate the comic relief. Just be sure to cue up the story in a warm, touching way in your note. Tell them how much the memory means to you, too!

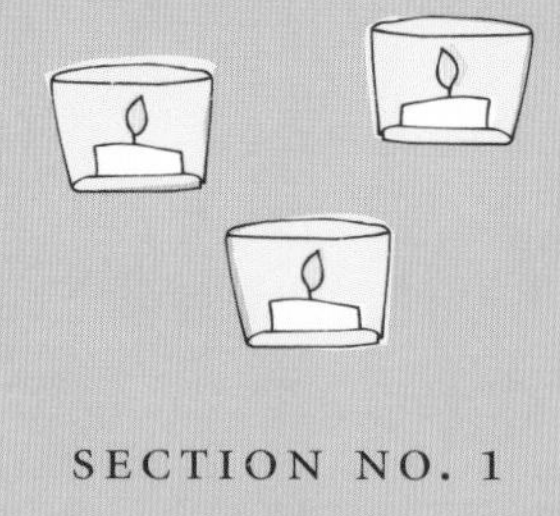

SECTION NO. 1

writing *sympathy* notes

While often a daunting task, writing a meaningful sympathy note is one of the most important acts of support we can offer people who are grieving. From reaching out with sympathy, offers of help, and care to sharing memories, stories, and heartfelt wishes, these notes help ease the pain of grieving people. When asked what they remember about periods of bereavement, people often cite notes from friends and family as reminders of love and caring that helped bring them through a dark and sad time. These notes are important, and with a little guidance, you'll start to see how much good your words can do for someone.

REASONS FOR SENDING

Sympathy

A sympathy note states that you've heard about the death and offers wishes, support, and thoughts to its recipient.

Sympathy Follow-Up

These notes support the grieving in the difficult, transitional months following a death. They fill a middle ground between sympathy and encouragement. They say you're still thinking about the recipient, are still there for her and still want to help. Consider including invitations to get together as well as enclosures like articles, photos, or gift cards for restaurants, movies, or other things she enjoys.

Consider sending sympathy follow-up notes anytime, but particularly on difficult days such as:

The deceased's or survivor's birthday.

A wedding anniversary (*to a grieving spouse*).

Christmas or other important holidays.

A time of year, day, or event that was important to the deceased.

The anniversary of the death.

Any other time a grieving person might need extra support.

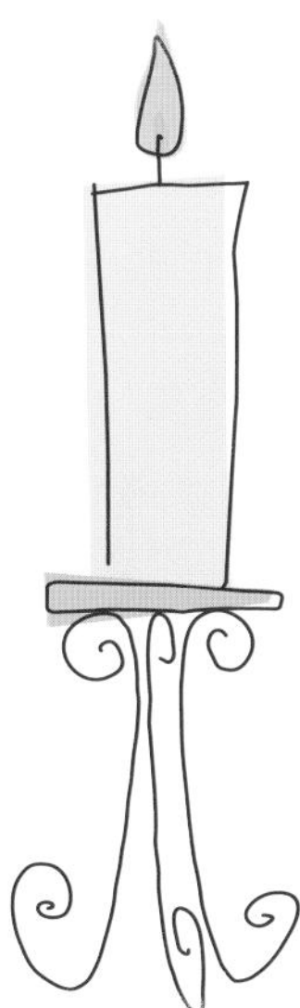

4 great *sympathy* notes

Mr. Hollings' note is addressed to the two surviving daughters of the deceased, so it seems likely that their mother has already died. Otherwise, the note probably would've been addressed to her. The sender has chosen to send the note after the funeral service—and turns its timing into an opportunity to compliment the funeral service.

Dear Valeria and Monica,

I would like to express my deep and heartfelt sympathy over the loss of your father. What a good and kindhearted man he was. I thought the funeral service was a wonderful tribute to him and to all he has done for our community. He will be missed by so many. I've been praying for your comfort and will continue to do so. Again, my deepest sympathy.

Sincerely,
Elmer Hollings

In this note, sensitivity and support work together to help Karen build her relationship with Hattie. It seems that the two are co-workers, neighbors, or other casual acquaintances. Karen mentions feeling a special connection to Hattie because she lost her husband to the same disease.

Dear Hattie,

I am so sorry to hear that Walter has died. I lost my husband to cancer, too, and my heart goes out to you now. Please know I'm thinking of you and wanting to do whatever I can to help. Can I bring a meal over sometime in the next week? I'll check in to see what day would work best for you. Until then, you're in my thoughts.

With deepest sympathy,
Karen Miller

WORTH NOTING: Karen mentions the word "cancer" but doesn't go into detail about the illness. She also doesn't presume to know how her recipient is feeling.

Dear Ron,

I just wanted to let you know you're in my thoughts, especially on the first anniversary of Helen's death. I can only imagine all you're feeling today, but I want you to know that I'm here for you every bit as much as I was a year ago. I'll give you a call to see if maybe you'd like to go get some pizza or take a bike ride.

Take good care of yourself. I'm thinking of you.

Your friend,
Tom

This perfect sympathy follow-up note from a friend recognizes the anniversary of a loved one's (*probably a wife's*) death. Tom's note achieves a nice balance of sympathy and encouragement and extends a warm, yet casual, offer to Ron to spend some time together.

Dear Mr. and Mrs. Green,

I am so very sorry about the loss of your daughter. Having spent four years at South High with Shauna, I have many good memories of her! She was a person who touched lives everywhere she went. I especially remember a volleyball trip our sophomore year when the bus broke down, and Shauna managed to get us all off the bus to watch the sun set. I've never known anyone quite like Shauna. My heartfelt sympathy goes out to you and your family. You're in my thoughts and prayers.

Sincerely,
Yolanda (Alvarez) Baker

This is a longish note that shares the kind of anecdote the deceased's parents are probably longing to hear. The Greens want and need to know that others thought Shauna was special and will miss her, too.

WORTH NOTING: Yolanda reminds her recipients of how she knew their daughter (from high school), which is important when you don't know the recipients well (or at all). She also includes her maiden name for recipients who might not know her by her married name.

writing your *sympathy* note

HAVE A LOOK AT THE QUESTIONS BELOW AND ANSWER AS MANY AS YOU CAN. YOUR ANSWERS WILL BE THE FOUNDATION OF YOUR NOTE:

How did you hear about the death? How did you feel?

What good things do you remember about the deceased?

What were some of his or her unique qualities?

Do you have an anecdote, memory, or funny story about the person that you think your recipient would appreciate or enjoy?

Will you or other people especially miss the person?

Is there anything that makes you especially remember or think of the deceased?

Are you thinking of or praying for your recipient?

What can you wish for them at this difficult time?

Would you like to do something specific to help out?

Have you lost someone? What did you want to hear?

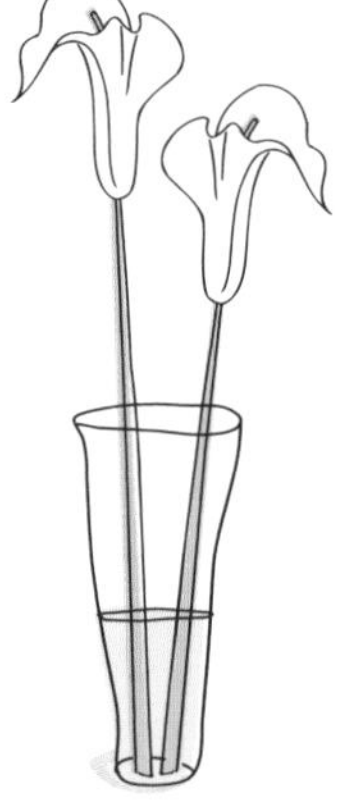

FOR MORE IDEAS
We've included additional sample notes at the end of this chapter.

Now, following the steps on pages 178-180, start to craft your note. Use your answers to these questions to guide you. For additional help, we've included some words and phrases on the following pages.

some of our favorite words for *sympathy* notes

YOUR FEELINGS:

Sorry	*Genuinely*	*Shocked*
Deeply	*Grieved*	*Truly*
Saddened	*Sincerely*	*Upset*

DESCRIBING THE DECEASED:

Kindhearted	*Talented*	*Admired*	*Unforgettable*
Considerate	*Well-Loved*	*Sweet*	*Respected*
One-of-a-Kind	*Honorable*	*Caring*	*Hardworking*

YOUR WISH FOR THE RECIPIENT:

Comfort	*Hope*	*Support*
Recovery	*Love*	*Solace*
Healing	*Rest*	*Memories*

a few great phrases for *sympathy* notes

I was so sorry to hear that (your sister) *passed away.*

Please accept my heartfelt sympathy on the loss of (Lou).

I'll never forget his story about (the runaway chicken).

I'll always remember the time when….

She was such a (kind and loving) *person.*

She was someone who (always had time to lend a hand).

(Your grandfather) *was so proud of you.*

Her (blueberry pie) *was the best.*

Our love and support are always here for you.

The weeks ahead will be (an adjustment), *and I want to help.*

I'd like to help you with (mowing the yard) *this weekend.**

*I'll give you a call Thursday, and we can set something up.**

**Be sure to follow through on anything you offer or promise.*

YOUR NOTE WILL BE COMFORTING WHEN...

Your recipient knows she's in your thoughts and prayers.

She knows she's not alone in missing her loved one.

She's able to smile at a fond memory you share.

a few extra pointers on *sympathy* notes

THINGS TO AVOID SAYING IN YOUR NOTE

As important as sympathy notes are, often the wrong words can send the wrong message to the grieving. While we have the best intentions, often some of the most tried and true phrases have a less than sympathetic tone when written in a note. Here is our short list of phrases to avoid and why.

I know how you feel. Even if you've experienced a similar loss, you risk minimizing your recipient's grief. Instead, try something like, "I've lost my husband, too, and I'm so sorry for you."

She's in a better place. He's at peace now. It's part of God's plan. Even if your recipient believes these things in her heart of hearts, they can be very difficult to hear and accept in the midst of grief, when the pain, injustice, and anger of death are in the forefront of her mind.

He lived a long, full life. She was so young. Avoid referring to the deceased's age. No matter whether it strikes the old or young, death is never welcome, expected, or easy to accept. Focus instead on what made the person memorable and special.

Anything that dwells on the details of an illness, death, accident, or manner of death. Again, focus on the person and, or communicating your caring and support to your recipient.

You should never have to bury a child. You never stop needing your mom. What a loss. Anything that might make your recipient feel worse.

*You should... You will...*Steer clear of expressing anything that may come off as too directive or presuming to tell the grieving what they will experience in coming weeks or months. Grieving people often feel very alone in their pain, and phrases such as these seem insensitive—as if the sender is minimizing or standardizing the pain and suffering.

Call me if there's anything I can do. The grieving are unlikely to take the initiative in asking for help. Instead, take the initiative for them and make a specific offer of support. Depending on timing and your relationship with the grieving, consider offering help with meals, housework, errands, child care, writing an obituary or thank-you notes, finalizing arrangements, etc. Even if they don't take you up on it right away, keep asking.

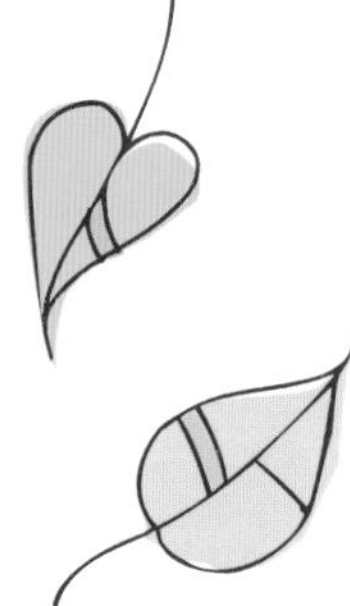

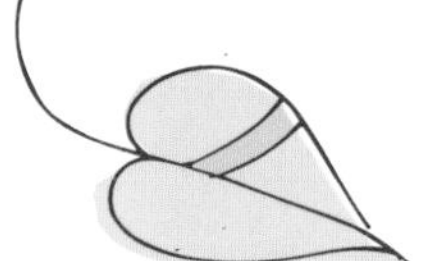

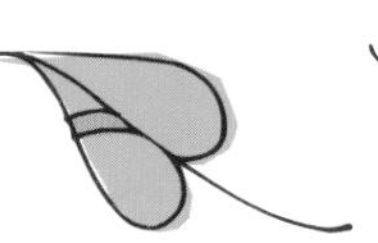

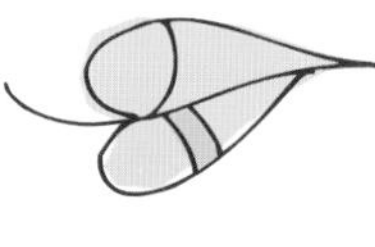

sample *sympathy* notes

FORMAL
DEATH OF CHILD

Dear Kyle and Tara,

I'd like to express my sincere sympathy over the loss of your son. My heart goes out to you both. In his time here, I know Martin was loved by so many. You and your family are in my thoughts and prayers. I'm very sorry for your loss.

Sincerely,
Mary Heinrich

PERSONAL
DEATH OF A
BELOVED RELATIVE

Dear Mr. Saint,

How very sorry I was to hear about your Aunt Olga's passing. She was always such a sweet lady—and a real character, too. I remember how she liked to have her fingernails painted in Springville's school colors during football season. We'll miss seeing her in the diner for coffee on Wednesdays. My thoughts and prayers are with you and your family at this difficult time.

With sympathy,
Myron Jackson

SUPPORTIVE
FROM COLLEAGUE
DEATH OF A PARENT

Dear Pam,

I am truly sorry to hear that your mother passed away. I know from the way you always talked about her that she meant a great deal to you, and I'm so sorry for your loss. Please don't worry about anything here at work. Abby and I have your responsibilities covered for as long as you need to be away. Just take good care of yourself and your family.

Once again, my deepest sympathy is with you right now.

Sincerely,
Margaret

Dear Ellen,

We were deeply saddened to hear the news of Jeremy's death in combat. We had the pleasure of talking with him at length last May at your parents' home, and we were so impressed with him as a person. We also have the highest respect for the sacrifice he made. Again, Ellen, we're so very sorry for your loss. May it be a comfort to know you're in our prayers.

With heartfelt sympathy,
Jim and Eva Myers

RESPECTFUL
DIFFICULT CIRCUMSTANCES
(ACCIDENT, COMBAT, CRIME)

Dear Mark,

Please accept our deepest sympathy in the loss of your beloved wife, Nancy. She was such a sweet, gentle presence in our neighborhood. We'll miss her beautiful flowers and having her stop to talk during her walks. We are praying that healing will touch your family's hearts right now.

Kate will be over tomorrow to look after Haley and Drew and can do so as often as you need in the weeks and months to come. Our thoughts, prayers, and heartfelt sympathy are with you and your family right now.

Your neighbors,
Pete and Eileen

COMPLIMENTARY
WITH OFFER OF HELP
DEATH OF SPOUSE

Dear Tony and Carla,

We know today is a tough day for you. McKenzie would have turned 30. Even after all these months, we know how very much you miss her. We miss her, too. You've both done such an inspiring job of turning your grief into helping others—you're a real inspiration to us all. We just wanted to let you know you're on our minds and in our hearts today.

Your friends,
Rich and Sylvia

PS: We'd love to have you over for dinner next Friday! We'll give you a call over the weekend to see if that's a good day. Sure hope so!

WARM FROM
CLOSE FRIENDS
SYMPATHY FOLLOW-UP

contents:

Business

Business or pleasure? Work or play? Many of us draw pretty strict lines between our 9-5 schedule and our life outside of work. However, some of our best practices from home can really work to our advantage at the office—like writing great notes.

To put it in business terms, the cost-benefit is in our favor. The cost (*time, effort, and supplies you'll put into writing notes*) is relatively low, while the benefit (*stronger professional relationships, for one*) can be immeasurably high. Clearly, the business case is there. And with a little practice, these notes can become a great way to mix business and pleasure!

CHAPTER INTRODUCTION

why *business* notes matter

As we all know, the working world operates at a fast and furious pace. Its tools of choice—phone calls, e-mails, and faxes—are aimed at getting the most done in the least amount of time. Handwritten notes are a distinct departure from all of that. Beyond the details of your message, the simple fact that you sat down and wrote a note communicates one very important thing to someone who receives it—*I took the time to write to you because you matter to me.* In a world of ever increasing efficiency, that message is priceless.

6 parts of a *business* note

No matter the occasion, business notes are made up of six distinct parts. Follow the steps outlined in this section and before you know it, you'll have your note signed, sealed, and delivered—and you'll make quick business of it, too.

①

Dear Mr. Cartwright,

②

I want to thank you so much for the bonus I received last Friday. It came as such a surprise! The past eight months have been very challenging, but also fulfilling for me, and it feels great to have my hard work recognized by a management group I respect so much. The hard work is far from over, and it really helps to know I have your support and encouragement. Thank you again.

③ ③ ④ ⑤ ④

⑥

Sincerely,
Alan Graves

① GREET THE RECIPIENT
② STATE WHY YOU'RE WRITING
③ ELABORATE
④ BUILD THE RELATIONSHIP & LOOK AHEAD
⑤ RESTATE THE REASON FOR WRITING
⑥ GIVE YOUR REGARDS

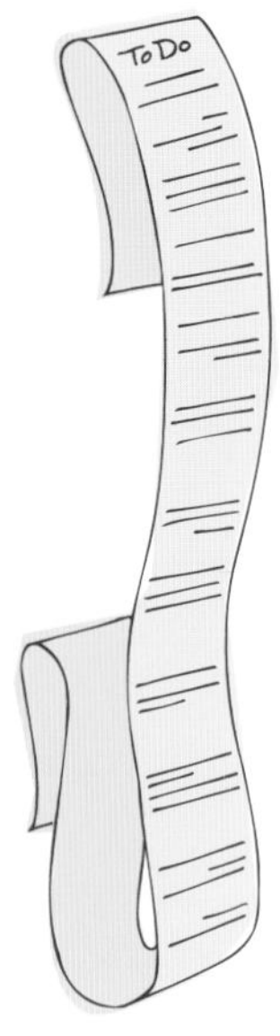

great *business* notes: step by step

① GREET THE RECIPIENT

In business, perhaps more than anywhere, first impressions matter. And so do second, third, and fiftieth impressions.

- If necessary, go to the extra trouble of confirming the spelling of first and last names.
- Use appropriate levels of formality—only use first names when you are 100% sure your recipient will be comfortable with it.

② STATE WHY YOU'RE WRITING

Business often involves reading a lot of correspondence in a short amount of time, so clarity and brevity count.

- State your point clearly and concisely.
- Make sure you make the purpose of your letter clear in the first line.

③ ELABORATE

Consider this your chance—in one to two sentences—to elaborate on the point you made in the first sentence.

- This is the place to personalize your notes. Include details and examples to bring your words to life.
- Give your reaction to, feelings about, or impression of the given topic.
- Show you know the recipients—speak to them, their skills, and their experience.

④ BUILD THE RELATIONSHIP & LOOK AHEAD

Look ahead and set a positive tone.

- Mention continued work together, a future meeting, or possible connection at a later date.
- When it comes to the future, be positive, not pushy.
- For notes of thanks, let the recipients know how much their help meant to you and extend an offer to help them in return in the future.

TIMING

Business rules tend to be a little less forgiving than social ones. The three-day rule applies strongly in this case. Try very hard to send your note within three days of the event or other occasion to be acknowledged, or within a week at most. Our advice—if more than two weeks have gone by, you might want to reconsider sending a note. It might be more conspicuous in its lateness than it would be if it weren't sent at all.

⑤ RESTATE YOUR REASON FOR WRITING

End your note by briefly mentioning again why you wrote.

- Use the end of your note as the chance to pack a punch with a warm, sincere, lighthearted, or upbeat rephrasing of what you expressed in the opening of your note.

⑥ GIVE YOUR REGARDS

- Generally, stick with formal, simple regards like *Sincerely* or *All the best.*
- For good friends or celebratory notes, consider warmer closings.

For a complete list of closings, see Great Endings on page 216.

SO THERE YOU HAVE IT...

Business notes are good for business relationships, and you don't need an MBA to write a great one. You can send them for many of the same reasons as you would other notes, and you can adapt the basic elements of almost any category of personal notes for business.

Now all that's left to do is get down to the business of writing!

memo: some information on *business* notes

BUSINESS NOTES CAN BE DIVIDED INTO TWO MAIN CATEGORIES:

Notes That Establish Relationships

These notes "get your foot in the door" in a professional, courteous way. They communicate that an initial meeting or other contact with the person has not been forgotten and that building a relationship is important to you.

Notes That Maintain Relationships

Just as personal notes can help you nurture your friendships and family relationships, business notes can help you take care of your professional connections. Taking the time to write a gracious note shows you care about maintaining the relationship.

CODE OF CONDUCT FOR BUSINESS NOTES

The building blocks for a great business note are the same as those for other notes discussed in this book. A thank-you note to a valued client will have the same basic elements as a thank-you note to a close friend. However, business notes do have their own unique considerations. When writing, keep in mind the following business-specific guidelines.

Remember Titles and Tone

Never does addressing your note properly count more than in business correspondence. Be sure that your note is addressed to reflect the relationship. When in doubt, be sure to use Mr., Ms., Mrs., Dr., Colonel, or other formal or professional titles.

Tone, too, matters in business. While you might feel very comfortable with your colleagues, maintaining professionalism with your language is very important. Remember that this is not a note to your sister or best friend, so be sure to keep your tone businesslike throughout.

Even with more casual business notes, keep in mind the difference between "casual" (jeans) and "business casual" (khakis). Make sure your notes are more khakis than jeans.

Don't Be Pushy

While it may be perfectly natural to suggest a lunch or future meeting with a friend or family member, be sure not to assume too much in matters of business correspondence. Sometimes a well placed, "I hope we can meet again soon to continue our discussion..." puts the invitation ball in your colleague's court without coming across as presumptuous, or worse, pushy!

Don't Intrude

In personal matters—such as family or marital issues, illness, legal issues, or job troubles—often a simple "Thinking of You" note lets your colleague know that you care without putting them on the spot. While many of us are open with our personal lives, some people really do guard their personal privacy. Your note needs to take that into consideration, especially during difficult, emotional, or potentially embarrassing times.

Don't Over-Promise

Though notes we send to colleagues, employees, business partners, and clients are often filled with compliments and relationship builders, be careful not to say or offer anything in your note that you won't be able to deliver. Remember, when it comes to messages in personal notes, be careful to walk your notes' talk.

THE EMOTIONAL VALUE OF BUSINESS NOTES

Truth be told, the business world can get pretty impersonal. The meetings and exchanges that occur in a professional context can leave us feeling like we matter less than the project, the sale, or whatever the case may be. By writing notes, we can let people know that they really do matter to us. Including meaningful details about their work, a conversation we've had with them, or what we enjoy about working together can help make a real human connection.

SECTION NO. 1

writing *business* notes

While our colleagues may expect just a quick "Congratulations!" e-mail or a "Hey, thanks!" at the water cooler, many occasions give us opportunities to rise above and beyond the expected—to make the extra effort and add our unique personal touches to our business communication. And just wait and see what a difference a little personal touch can make!

REASONS FOR SENDING

The business world can be viewed much like our personal lives—with a varied range of situations where notes are great ways to add a personal touch and maintain relationships. Some areas of particular consideration when it comes to business include:

Thank-You Notes for gifts, supplies, favors, leads, referrals, bonuses, extra opportunities, above-and-beyond work, encouragement, support, advice, or mentoring.

Support Notes for sympathy, get well, difficult project, interpersonal issues, job loss, or other professional or personal problems.

Notes for Special Days or Events like work anniversaries or milestones, birthdays, holidays, degrees received, objectives met, or projects completed.

Congratulatory Notes for Achievements such as a promotion, winning a client, big sale, job well done, or life events like a marriage, baby, adoption, or a child's graduation.

Keeping in Touch Notes to say hello, remind associates you're available, let customers know you appreciate their business, acknowledge an upcoming meeting, or just keep you top of mind with colleagues and associates.

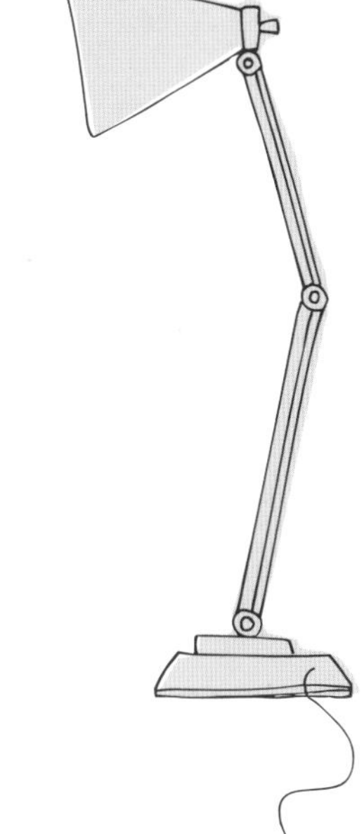

4 great *business* notes

This is a highly appreciative and complimentary thank-you note from a job interviewee to a potential employer. Enthusiasm and specific detail let Mr. Baker know that his firm made an impression on Lynette and that she is very interested in continuing discussions. Not pushy, this note puts the ball in Mr. Baker's court.

Dear Mr. Baker,

Thank you so much for taking the time to talk with me when I dropped off my portfolio on Wednesday. I've since had the chance to review the materials you gave me, and I am very impressed with the vision, creativity, and quality of the work. I was particularly impressed with the thoughtful and original way your firm handled the Johnston's Soup account. I would be thrilled to come in again at your convenience to talk about how my past experience and creative skills might most meet the needs of your firm. I hope to talk with you again soon.

Sincerely,
Lynette Franklin

Kevin's sympathy note to his colleague, Cynthia, comes across as personal yet still appropriately respectful. She is sure to appreciate hearing that he remembers her speaking highly of her grandfather and the things he taught her.

Dear Cynthia,

I was sorry to learn of the loss of your grandfather this week. In the time you and I have worked together, I have heard you speak so highly of him. In fact, I particularly remember the story of how he taught you to fly fish when you were young. Please know that my thoughts and prayers are with you at this difficult time.

Sincerely,
Kevin Jones

Dear Anna,

Warmest congratulations on your well-deserved promotion! It's a real pleasure seeing you receive this kind of recognition. Your work is always fresh, innovative, and right on target. Our firm is lucky to have someone as talented as you on board. Again, congratulations. I know this is only the beginning of many good things to come for you and your career!

Sincerely,
Barbara Miller

Here's a hearty pat on the back that Anna can keep, complete with meaningful compliments about past performance and high hopes for future success. It clearly comes from someone of authority—note how Ms. Miller has signed her last name. Clearly, Anna does not usually get notes from her, so this seems to be a big, noteworthy occasion.

Dear Lorraine,

Happy Birthday! I just wanted to drop you a note on your special day to let you know I'm thinking of you. I hope this year is filled with the things you enjoy the most—and I hope you'll have some time to go enjoy some sushi this weekend to celebrate. I also want to let you know how much I've enjoyed working with you this year. Your enthusiasm, energy, and optimism are contagious, and it's amazing what a positive influence you've had on the whole department. Thanks so much for being you—have a wonderful birthday!

Cheers,
Michelle

Michelle's warm birthday note to Lorraine takes advantage of an opportunity to express appreciation for their working relationship as well as Lorraine's unique contributions. Michelle really shows her knowledge of the recipient by mentioning a favorite food and specifying traits that have made a positive impact at work. What a great way to honor someone on her special day!

writing your *business* note

IN ORDER TO MAKE SURE THAT YOUR NOTE IS MEETING ALL ITS OBJECTIVES, ASK YOURSELF THESE QUESTIONS BEFORE PUTTING PEN TO PAPER:

What is the occasion or reason for writing?

Why is this person—and the relationship—important to you?

If a new acquaintance, did you enjoy meeting her?

If an existing relationship, how long have you worked together?

What admirable qualities does the person have?

What do you like about working with her?

Is there a specific interaction with her that you can mention?

What would she most like to hear right now?

What details can you include to let the person know you really remember her and her work?

Ultimately, what do you hope to accomplish with your note?

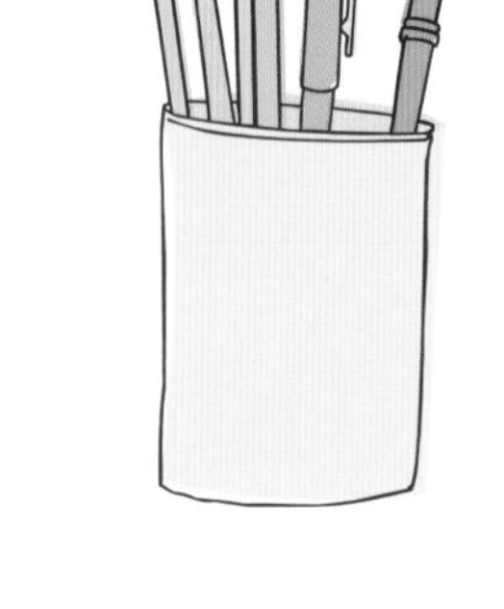

MEMORANDUM
Additional samples of some great business notes are included at the end of this chapter.

Now, following the steps outlined on pages 198–200, use your answers to these questions, along with some of the words and phrases on the following pages, to guide you through writing your note. Bet you'll have the whole deal wrapped up in no time.

some of our favorite words for *business* notes

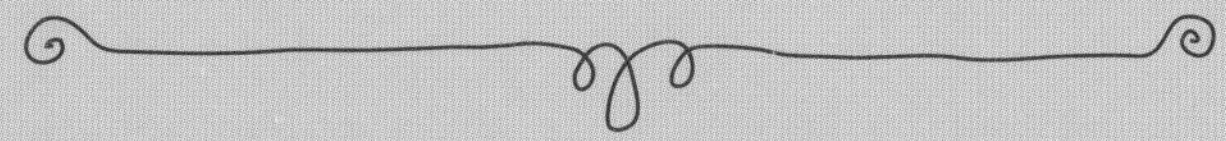

DESCRIBING YOU:

Impressed	*Thankful*	*Committed*	*Appreciative*
Grateful	*Pleased*	*Glad*	*Confident*
Interested	*Sorry*	*Fortunate*	*Optimistic*

DESCRIBING THE RECIPIENT:

Professional	*Capable*	*Insightful*	*Respected*
Dedicated	*Talented*	*Pleasant*	*Valued*
Cooperative	*Efficient*	*Creative*	*Enthusiastic*

DESCRIBING THE RECIPIENT'S WORK:

Impressive	*Productive*	*Thorough*	*Important*
Engaging	*Thoughtful*	*Promising*	*Well-Respected*
Top Notch	*Provocative*	*Unique*	*Significant*

a few great phrases for *business* notes

My sincere (congratulations) *on* (your recent promotion).

I was (very interested) *to learn about…*

I'm so glad you took the time (to meet with us).

I've been very impressed by your work, especially…

I've appreciated your (flexibility) *through all of this.*

Working with you is always (such a pleasure).

You always have such a (positive, energetic, optimistic) *attitude.*

Your (presentation) *was very* (thorough and engaging).

Your (business success) *is no surprise to me.*

You should be proud of (all you've accomplished).

Our (meeting) *was one of the most* (productive) *we've had!*

I'm grateful for the opportunity to (discuss the position you need to fill).

YOUR NOTE'S A GREAT PERFORMER WHEN...

Colleagues and associates are impressed that you took the time to write a note when all they expected was a quick e-mail.

They know that you truly appreciate their hard work, phone call, or loyalty.

They feel affirmed as professionals, colleagues, or individuals and confident about the future of your working relationship.

sample notes for *business*

GRACIOUS
THANK YOU FOR HELP

Dear Lydia,

I'm writing to thank you for agreeing to mentor me as I make the transition to your department. I was so pleased when you said you'd be happy to help me because I really admire your work and value your experience. I know you have a lot of great knowledge to share, and I look forward to learning from you. Thank you again!

Sincerely,
Casey Karlson

FRIENDLY & UPBEAT
THANKS FOR BUSINESS

Dear Mrs. Anderson,

Thank you so much for your recent order. I'm so glad to see that my favorite Odds 'n' Ends customers like my new summer designs! I remembered how much you liked the Little Daisy frame last time we met, so I've included an extra one in your order for you to keep. Please don't hesitate to contact me if you have any questions or concerns about this order or future ones. Thanks for your business!

Sincerely,
Erica Wilson

WARM & APPRECIATIVE
THANK YOU
FOR REFERRAL

Sean,

I wanted to take a minute to thank you for introducing me to George Smith. One of our web applications is a perfect fit for his business! It seems like you're always on the lookout for ways to help out a fellow businessman, and I hope you know how much I appreciate that. Please give me a call next time you're in town—I'd like the chance to take you to lunch to thank you properly! Also, please give my best to Joann.

With thanks,
Harold Meyers

Hi Carlie,

I just want to express my ongoing support as you continue your work on the Bateman account. I know this has been a long and sometimes frustrating project, and I really appreciate the positive attitude you've demonstrated from the very beginning. Please don't hesitate to ask for whatever you need during the next few weeks, whether it's working off-site or flex time—especially after some of those late-night conference calls. I'm confident we're going to wrap this up with great results very soon, so thanks for hanging in there.

Sincerely,
Mark

SUPPORTIVE ACKNOWLEDGMENT OF HARD WORK

Dear Mr. and Mrs. McClain,

My sincere congratulations on the 5th anniversary of Kids Kuts. It hardly seems like five years ago that I was stocking your product shelves for the first time! What a pleasure it's been working with you and watching your business grow. It just goes to show what great people can do with a great concept. Congratulations on five fabulous and well-earned years of success!

Sincerely,
Sue Unruh

CONGRATULATORY FOR BUSINESS SUCCESS

Richard,

Congratulations to you and Marie on the birth of Emily Nicole! I've forwarded the pictures to everyone in the office, and we're all in agreement: She's precious! I hope you enjoy these next few weeks at home with your new baby girl. Congratulations, Dad!

Sincerely,
Liza

SIMPLE & WARM BIRTH OF A CHILD

PS

some useful information for *note writing*

There you have it. And there it is...almost.

In this book, we've walked you through the process of writing great notes for eight of life's most important kinds of event-driven and emotionally driven sending needs. In each chapter, we've given you the six steps of a great note, provided a variety of sample notes, asked questions to get you thinking about your own notes and listed some of our favorite words and phrases to use. We've suggested expected—and unexpected—reasons for writing notes and we've talked about timing, special rules and other considerations so your notes are always in great taste. But some people just want more...

So, OK...here it is. For those of you who can't get enough of our help, we've included additional information in this section, which we have cleverly named our "PS" section. Maybe you'll read it now, maybe you'll wait until later, but whenever you get to it, we think you'll like it.

We cover topics like great endings for all occasions, paper choice, envelope addressing, and what people will think if you just up and start writing great notes. We've also added our "Ready-for-Anything Note-Writing Checklist" on the last page of this chapter, so you can be sure you're ready, no matter what kind of note-necessitating curveball life throws you.

You can thank us later.

great *endings* for personal notes

REGARDS

Most of the example notes in this book—as well as those we all write—tend to close with the safe, all-purpose, "Sincerely." All-purpose regards are great since they can be used for anyone from a friend to a business contact you haven't yet met in person. However, for closer relationships, for specific emotional needs, or just for flair, consider closing your note with one of the regards included below.

Family and Close Friends: Fondly, Warmly, Yours truly, Lovingly, Love, Lots of love, My/Our love, With love, Your son, Your friend, Your loving (mother), Your devoted (sister).

Gratitude: Gratefully, Gratefully yours, With thanks, With gratitude, With deepest gratitude, With love and gratitude, Your grateful (friend), My thanks, Many thanks, Appreciatively, Thankfully yours.

Congratulations: My/Our sincere congratulations, My/Our heartfelt congratulations, With warmest congratulations, With admiration, With love and pride, Good for you!

Romantic Love: Love, My love, All my love, My love forever, I love you, Yours, Yours always, Forever/Eternally yours, Always, Tenderly, Passionately, Affectionately, XOXOXO, Your loving (wife).

Apology: My apologies, My sincere apologies, Truly sorry, Sincerely sorry.

Comfort and Cheer: Thinking of you, With warmest thoughts, With caring thoughts, With warmest wishes, With hope, With hope and warm thoughts.

Sympathy: With sympathy, With deepest sympathy, In sympathy, My/Our condolences.

Religious: God bless, Blessings, Bless you, My/Our love and prayers, With hope and prayers, In Him, In His name, In His love.

Business: Regards, Best regards, Best wishes, All the best, Yours, Yours truly, With thanks.

SOME CONVENTIONS FOR REGARDS

When choosing your regards, try to avoid repeating anything already written in the body of the note. For example, if your note begins, "Please accept my deepest sympathy" then "With deepest sympathy" is repetitive as a closing. "Sincerely" or "My condolences" would be a better choice in this case.

The general rule is to capitalize only the first word of your regards. Subsequent words should start with a lowercase letter unless they would normally be capitalized. Follow your regards with a comma. For example:

Best wishes, Richard	Yours, Elena	Fondly, madly, truly, Frank

BUCKING CONVENTION

Feel free to use a regard of your own invention or to skip the regards altogether and just sign your name. It's your note, after all, so do what feels right.

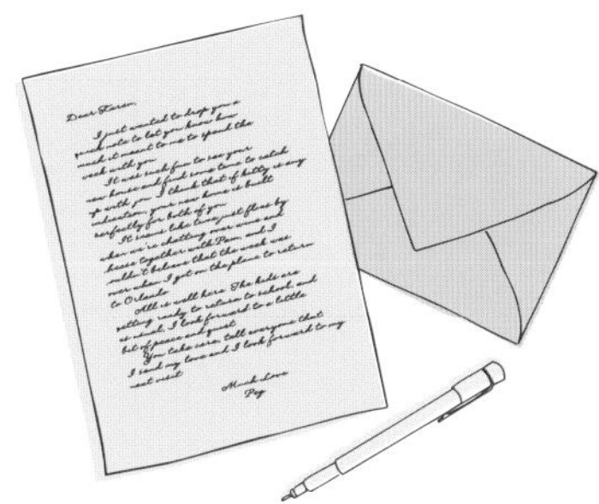

choosing *papers* for your personal notes

CHOOSING GREAT PAPERS FOR YOUR NOTES

Handwritten notes are among the most personal kinds of correspondence that you can send, and the paper you choose not only sets the tone for your note, but also says a lot about you, your style, and your tastes—not to mention the note's occasion and your relationship with the recipient. Some examples include the following.

Paper can reflect your personality

Like dogs? Send paw prints or an animal charity card.

Proud of your Irish heritage? Consider four-leaf clover imagery.

Are you mad for purple? Let your purple paper announce it's from you!

Your relationship with the recipient

If you often meet for coffee, look for a café design.

Thank-you for a dinner party? Maybe a wine scene would be just the thing.

Are you both chocoholics? Consider paper with candies or cake on it.

The occasion

For holidays, seasonal imagery can really amplify your happy wishes.

For birthdays, consider balloons, confetti, or bright color.

For occasions, consider using paper with colors that reflect the season.

The tone of the note

Mostly, it's good to play with fun notes for more casual sending situations.

For business, sympathy, or other more formal notes, stick with something a little more understated. In fact, a simple paper with little to no design is best.

OUR 3 FAVORITE NOTE-WRITING PAPERS

Letter Sheets—a 7 1/4" x 10 1/2" single sheet that folds in thirds vertically to fit inside a matching envelope for more casual notes and letters. Think of these as stationery sheets. They're a good choice for longer notes.

Correspondence Cards—These are usually a 4 1/4" x 6 1/4" single, unfolded panel of heavy cardstock. Often monogrammed or imprinted with initials or a full name, they can also include simple borders and limited accent design. They fit unfolded into envelopes but can often also be used as a postcard for more casual sending needs. Correspondence cards are gaining in popularity because of versatility and ease of use.

Fold-Over Notes—Size varies. These fold along the top or left side and may be blank or have artwork or printed messages such as "Thank You" and "Hello" on their fronts. They are by far the most popular form of notes—easy to find and keep on hand.

personalizing your notes

BE PERSONAL

Just as your words will certainly be uniquely yours, your notepaper can be, too! Consider just a few ways to add a little more "you" to your notes.

Monogramming and Personalization

Consider investing in personalized stationery products—from fold-over notes to letter sheets. Many computer programs allow you to print your name on card-stock using home printers. Personalized and monogrammed papers can also be professionally printed for you by stationery suppliers.

Preprinted Initials

Notes with initials printed on them are great ways to add personality without going to the expense and trouble of fully personalized products. Many such notes are available in stores and online.

Embossers

Embossing tools allow you to personalize any paper product—from notes to sheets to envelopes—and are very easy to use. They can be ordered with name, address, or other personal information and designs.

Stickers and Seals

Stickers and seals are a great way to add a little something extra to notes and envelopes. Consider having a variety on hand. Just be sure you use them for casual, celebratory, and fun events. Business and formal sending needs pretty much rule them out.

Handwritten Embellishments

Smiley faces. Little squiggly drawings. Lots of exclamation points. You can have fun with the content of your note by using your imagination (*and your pen*) to add extra energy to your notes. Just be sure the occasion, the tone, and the recipient call for your extra touch!

DOES MY NOTE LOOK PERSONAL?

Put your note to this test. Will the recipient guess it's from you before she even opens it? If not, what could you do to make sure she can?

some *envelope* how-tos

TIPS & TRICKS

Although the content of your note should get the vast majority of your attention, the envelope it arrives in can help make a great first impression. While some people will argue for the "art" of addressing personal correspondence, the fact is there are many different ways to make sure your envelope and note share the same tone and overall feeling. Some of our favorite tips and tricks are listed below.

How did you address your note? Your envelope should have the same level of formality as the note itself.

> For example, for a note that begins *Dear Dr. and Mrs. Lawrence*, the name line on the envelope should read *Dr. and Mrs. William Lawrence*. First names should be used on the envelope but not on the note itself.
>
> For a casual note that begins *Hi, Jack!*, consider a simple name line of Jack Thomas.
>
> For a note to a couple and their family that begins *Dear Richard and Georgia, We're wishing you and your family*...consider several different options, and pick the one that feels best for you!
>
> > Some possibilities include:
> > The Montgomery Family
> > Richard and Georgia Montgomery
> > Richard, Georgia, Leo, and Trudy Montgomery

Consider bright, fun envelopes as ways to really make your note stand out in the mail stack! Of course, keep in mind that certain occasions, such as sympathy, business, or wedding thank-you, as well as certain relationships, call for more restraint.

There's just something about seeing your name written, so avoid using printed address labels on envelopes for handwritten notes. Take the time to make your envelope as personal as your note!

ENVELOPE ADDRESSING 101

The information needed on an envelope that is mailed includes:

Recipient's Name
Recipient's Address (*Number, Street, Apartment Number*)
Recipient's City and State (*Use full spelling of state or correct abbreviation*)
Recipient's ZIP Code
Recipient's Country (*if other than the country from which the note is mailed*)

Your return address needs to be on the envelope, too. Both the upper left hand corner of the front of the envelope and the back flap of the envelope are correct places for return addresses. A few examples:

Lydia and Carl Jacobs
823 Spencer Road
St. Charles, MO 63303

Mr. & Mrs. Roland Thompson
1012 Saint Thomas Road
Atlanta, GA 30301

The Carver Family
300 Mountainview Drive
Boulder, CO 80301

Miss Mikaela Johnston
15 Grand Street
Apt. 4C
Hoboken, NJ 07030

Amie Lynn DeSoto
Franklin Department Store
1 Allen Way
Charlotte, VA 28216

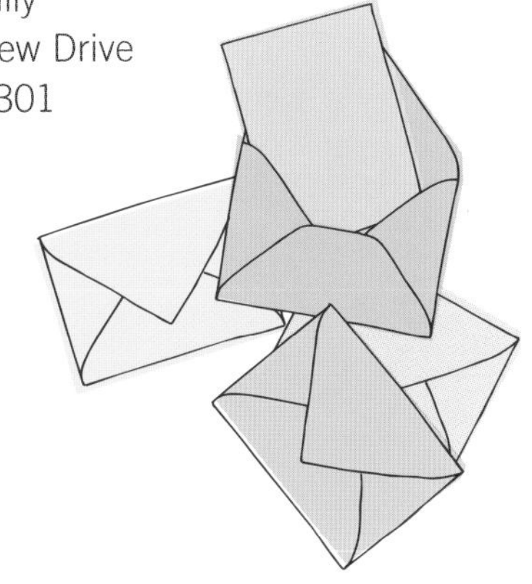

On an envelope that is hand-delivered, the only information that needs to be on it is the recipient's name.

some *note-writing* questions answered

Why not send a greeting card instead of a note? People expect them from me, especially for birthdays, holidays, and other occasions.

Does a carpenter use only a hammer to build a house? Nope. Does a chef use just a knife to cook with? Hardly. So why limit yourself to one form of communication? Exactly...You shouldn't, and you sure don't have to.

Like notes, greeting cards are a great way to reach out to friends and family, acknowledge important occasions, and nurture connections. And the good news is that even when the occasion or recipient calls for a greeting card, you can use the basics you've learned in this book to make the messages you write in your greeting cards better, too. Just work with the space available, and use the same basic "anatomy" you would use for a personal note.

But remember—the greeting card you choose is likely to state your reason for writing (*a birthday card will say "birthday," for example*), so you might be able to skip a step or two that you would normally need to cover in your note. Just be sure to elaborate on the greeting card's message, and use the note you write inside as your chance to talk one-on-one with its recipient. See what feels right for you. And remember—notes and greeting cards are both great tools to keep in your communication toolbox!

I have the handwriting of a third grader. Should I even consider writing notes?
If you're unhappy with your handwriting, first consider the possibility that you're just being your own toughest critic. What seems bad to you might (*and probably does*) look just fine to anyone else. Plus, people really care about what you're saying, as opposed to how good your handwriting is (*or isn't*).

That said, if you're still pretty sure your handwriting makes chicken scratch look good, try this—Relax.

Write a rough draft of your note, and focus on making each word legible. Try practicing writing slowly and carefully, and see if that doesn't make a difference.

If that doesn't do the trick, consider...
You might want to write your notes on paper (*as opposed to note cards*) and lay guide lines underneath. Most sheets of lined paper will show through enough to help keep the lines of your note from sloping too badly.

Think about printing instead of using script. Since we write printed letters one at a time, printing has a way of at least making things legible.

If you still think your handwriting is too hopeless, you can type your notes as a last resort. But do include a signature from your own hand. It's OK for those to be messy, as long as your note's recipient knows it's from you!

I haven't written many notes in the past. Will people think I'm weird if I start now?
You might think it will seem strange to people who know you if you suddenly start writing lots of nice notes thanking them, congratulating them, or just saying hi. And it might at first, but ask yourself this: Is this the kind of change they're likely to complain about? That said, you might want to start out slowly. Send a nice thank-you note the first time you have a reason. Then send a little "just because" love note to your significant other. See what kind of difference that makes. We think you'll wish you started sending notes sooner! So be confident about turning over a new leaf (*or note card*) and just start writing!

the ready-for-anything *note-writing* checklist

Make sure you've got all the necessary supplies on hand for whatever note-writing event—or inspiration—comes your way.

A COLLECTION OF NOTE CARDS AND PAPER and matching envelopes in enough variety to cover a range of potential sending occasions from celebratory to serious.

AN UPDATED ADDRESS BOOK, whether paper or electronic.

POSTAGE STAMPS with a variety of designs (*to cover a range of occasions from formal to festive*) and denominations (*for everything from postcards to heavy notes with photos or other enclosures*).

A LIST of birthdays, anniversaries, spouses' and kids' names, and other information you won't want to hunt for when you need it.

A SELECTION OF PENS to add variety to your handwriting and your notes.

A DICTIONARY AND THESAURUS, so you've got spelling and vocabulary help within easy reach.

PRACTICE PAPER to list ideas and sketch out a draft version of your note before you put pen to real notepaper.

A VARIETY OF EMBELLISHMENTS like stickers and seals, to add personality to your notes and envelopes.

OUR LAST 2¢ WORTH

1. Be Realistic

You're not going to turn into a note-writing Olympian overnight. Nobody expects that, and you'll just stress yourself out trying. Instead, consider approaching it like any new skill-based endeavor—start slowly, and build up.

Over time, you'll find your note-writing muscles tightening and reflexes getting sharper. And you'll also learn to tell when enough's enough. Start by promising yourself you'll write one great note this week, whether for a birthday or "just because." Next week, aim for two. Soon, it will come naturally.

2. Be Yourself

Notes give you the chance to express yourself. Not some super-shiny, high-falutin', putting-on-airs you, but the real, genuine, full-of-personality-and-style-and-even-some-misspellings you. So don't be tempted to be overly affected in your notes—just be real. And once you get a few great notes under your belt, you'll be amazed what emotional range you possess.

So, there they are—all the basics you need to write a great note for any occasion.

And with some practice and plenty of your own creativity, you'll be writing great notes in no time.
All we have left to say is....Enjoy!

about the *authors*

This book was written by two real people who have some experience of their own with note writing. And life. And other stuff, too.

Recently in her adventurous life, Angela Ensminger realized the value and fun of note writing. Despite her mother's best attempts to teach her the importance of written correspondence, Angela never had much time to write notes when she was younger. With jobs as varied as Peace Corps volunteer in Morocco to Travel Writer in New York, she was always on the go...and who could figure the postage anyway?

Then she moved to Kansas City, fell in love, and got married on a beach in Jamaica. But because there were all those wedding thank-you notes to write, the honeymoon was over pretty quickly. So figuring that writing all those notes couldn't be harder than learning to speak Arabic, she plunged in pen first and realized there was something to this note-writing thing, after all. And when it was all said and done, she thought maybe someone else would like to know how to do this, too. Thus, this book was born.

Now that the wedding thank-yous have been sent, Angela can focus on being an Editorial Director for Hallmark. She can also be found at home in Kansas City, hanging out with her husband, Aaron, and their herd of cats.

Keely Chace was always a wordsmith, but rarely a note writer. In fact, if anyone had told a younger Keely that she would one day author a book about note writing, she would have laughed. Or at least thought the notion a little odd. She was too busy enjoying life in rural Kansas and her lifelong pastimes—reading and obsessing about her thighs. She would have penned a sonnet before a thank-you note any day. But things can change…and they did.

After getting married and later having a daughter, Keely learned a thing or two about writing great notes. From "Thanks for the blender!" to "Olivia loves the swing!", Keely cranked out note after note—even though they were often decorated with strained peas. And this book is filled with Keely's hard-won lessons in note writing.

When not writing Mother's Day verse or a happy wish for a birthday card, Keely, a senior Hallmark Writer, can be found tackling endless fix-up projects at home in Kansas City with her husband, Jason, and teaching her daughter Olivia, now 2, how to write the alphabet. Teaching Olivia how to write great notes will have to wait a couple of years.

WRITE US!

If you've enjoyed this book, we'd love to hear from you. Practice your note writing skills and send your comments to:

Book Feedback
2501 McGee, Mail Drop 215
Kansas City, MO 64141-6580

Or e-mail us at:
booknotes@hallmark.com